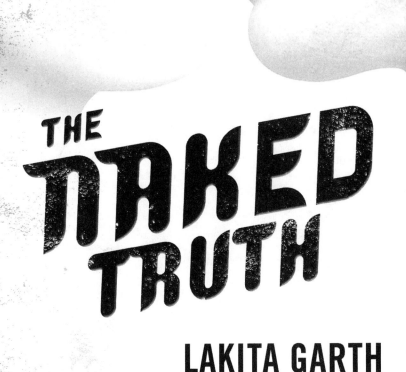

THE NAKED TRUTH

LAKITA GARTH

Regal

From Gospel Light
Ventura, California, U.S.A.

Published by Regal Books
From Gospel Light
Ventura, California, U.S.A.
Printed in the U.S.A.

Regal Books is a ministry of Gospel Light, a Christian publisher dedicated to serving the local church. We believe God's vision for Gospel Light is to provide church leaders with biblical, user-friendly materials that will help them evangelize, disciple and minister to children, youth and families.

It is our prayer that this Regal book will help you discover biblical truth for your own life and help you meet the needs of others. May God richly bless you.

For a free catalog of resources from Regal Books/Gospel Light, please call your Christian supplier or contact us at 1-800-4-GOSPEL *or* www.regalbooks.com.

Library of Congress Cataloging-in-Publication Data
Garth, Lakita.
The naked truth / Lakita Garth.
p. cm.
ISBN 0-8307-4328-6 (hard cover)
1. Sex—Religious aspects—Christianity. 2. Sex instruction for teenagers—Religious aspects—Christianity. I. Title.
BT708.G378 2006
241'.660835—dc22 2006037808

1 2 3 4 5 6 7 8 9 10 / 10 09 08 07

Rights for publishing this book in other languages are contracted by Gospel Light Worldwide, the international nonprofit ministry of Gospel Light. Gospel Light Worldwide also provides publishing and technical assistance to international publishers dedicated to producing Sunday School and Vacation Bible School curricula and books in the languages of the world. For additional information, visit www.gospellightworldwide.org; write to Gospel Light Worldwide, P.O. Box 3875, Ventura, CA 93006; or send an e-mail to info@gospellightworldwide.org.

Contents

CHAPTER 1 4
Madea Ain't Got Nothin' on My Mom

CHAPTER 2 21
The Naked Truth

CHAPTER 3 31
It Can't Happen to Me

CHAPTER 4 49
America's Most Unwanted

CHAPTER 5 71
I'll Just Practice Safe Sex

CHAPTER 6 88
They're Going to Do It Anyway

CHAPTER 7 95
What Two People Do Behind Closed Doors . . .

CHAPTER 8 108
It Just Happened

CHAPTER 9 119
I Just Listen to the Beat

CHAPTER 10 133
Peer Pressure/Everybody's Doing It

CHAPTER 11 143
It's Too Late for Me

CHAPTER 12 152
Marriage Is Just a Piece of Paper

APPENDIX 169
Self-Defense Manual

ENDNOTES 171

CHAPTER 1

Madea Ain't Got Nothin' on My Mom

No one from the old neighborhood I was born in ever thought I'd be a model or Miss Black California. They never thought I'd be featured on television shows or major magazines, including *Vogue*, *Essence*, *People* and *Glamour*. They never thought I'd hang out with stars or senators or ambassadors or heads of state—let alone become the founder and CEO of my own company. You see, that's not what people in my neighborhood expected out of life. I was born in one of *Money* magazine's "most dangerous places to live" and "worst places to raise children" in America. But at the time, I didn't know any different. I just knew it as home.

My mom became a single parent after my dad died of cancer. (So yes, I know who my daddy is, thank you very much.) She was left with the responsibility of raising my four older brothers—Kevin, David, Leon and Mark—and me. We didn't grow up with a lot of material things. We were often the last kids to get anything cool. I remember when Members Only jackets were the "in" thing—I think I was one of the very last Members. If I wanted a "swish" on the side of my tennis shoes, I had to draw it on with a Sharpie ™ marker. You know you're poor when your shoes don't come in a box, but instead come with the shoestrings tied together in a grocery store bin. We really didn't care. We were just grateful to get new shoes.

As far as fashion, we let our pants hang low long before it was ever popular in the hip-hop scene. We didn't do it because it looked cool. We purposely bought our pants too big as a matter of economics so that when we grew, our pants wouldn't flood and they would still fit. I remember that my brothers had these crazy growth spurts. One summer a couple of them grew four to six inches in just a few months. Let's just say it's not cool for a "brotha" to wear capris.

Besides providing for us, my mom was also responsible for protecting us. If you've ever seen *Diary of a Mad Black Woman* or *Madea's Family Reunion*, then you'll understand: Madea ain't got nothing on my mom! Everybody on the block knew that she slept with two men every night: Smith and Wesson. Only that's no joke! She would shoot you if you broke into her house or touched one of her kids.

I remember one time when I came home from school, Mom was busy watering the lawn and the guys across the street were playing basketball. During a conversation with the guys, she told them, "You know, boys, I keep a gun with me at all times and there are only two things I'd ever kill you over. First, if you break into my house and the second is if you touch my daughter."

The boys didn't hesitate to answer, "Yes, Mrs. Garth." Consequently, our house was the only house on the block that was never broken into—and you can bet that no one ever touched her daughter.

Together my mom and dad were a force to be reckoned with. Our house definitely had some rules, boundaries and guidelines. My dad had served in the Air Force for 27 years and fought in World War II, Korea and Vietnam. He died of cancer when I was 11. They think it was from Agent Orange. While he was alive, he was a very strict disciplinarian. If Dad couldn't bounce a quarter off your bed, he would strip it down to the mattress, and he would keep doing this for as many times as it took for you to figure out how to make your bed. It didn't take long to learn.

Among my friends, we were often the butt of jokes—not because we didn't wear the latest styles—but because Mom's rules were so strict. One of my mom's big rules was *Be in the house when the streetlights come on*. When those lights came on, we instantly transformed into the U.S. Olympic Track and Field Team. We'd jump over hedges, fences, puddles, trashcans and animals—whatever it took to get home. We couldn't move faster than the speed of light, but we were close to the speed of sound, because we were in her sight and into her house before she finished her sentence.

In some neighborhoods, being outside when the streetlights come on means you might catch a cold, but in my neighborhood, it meant that you might catch a bullet. You could get involved in gang activity, drug activity and a lot of other unpleasant activities, so when my mother said be somewhere at a certain time, there were reasons why.

We might not have understood the reasons at the time, and sometimes we might not have gotten a reason even if we had asked. We were just expected to obey. Oh, for joy! Mom wasn't trying to cut in on our fun. She used to say, "I'm not trying to be mean. I just mean what I say." Mom gave us rules like *Be in the house when the streetlights come on* because she loved us, because she didn't want us to get hurt, and because she knew and wanted something better for us.

Even today, when I drive around certain neighborhoods that don't have streetlights, I can't help but wonder, *How do you know when to come home?*

Impressionable minds live up to the expectations placed on them.

Mom wasn't just concerned about us following the rules. She also had an eye on our futures. She cared what happened to us and she wasn't afraid to remind us of where we were headed. She made sure that the whole family was future-oriented. Where would we go after elementary school? Middle school. Where we would go after middle school? High school. And where would we go after high school? Out of Momma's house, because she couldn't wait to be an empty nester!

Mom had different expectations than other parents. She made sure we all had a plan for what to do after high school, whether it was college or the military. Mom taught us that impressionable minds live up to the expectations placed on them, and she knew that if she didn't raise us right the first time, then she'd end up raising us the rest of her life. Meanwhile, we knew we didn't want to be thirty-somethings still living in our momma's basement. That's why she made sure we earned good grades in school, and she sacrificed herself to make sure we did. Many times these days, you can't get a parent to show up at a PTA (Parent Teacher Association) meeting, but my mom was always there. She would take off from work to be at those meetings, whether or not they docked her pay. Once she was there, she didn't just make sure to meet every teacher—she would ask them to assign us extra work!

We used to watch our mom get up while it was still dark to go to work. If we needed cleats or a dance lesson or anything to further our education or development, she would sacrifice so that we could have those things. She never had the latest clothes or flashy jewelry. While we were growing up, she never spent money on a makeup, nail or hair appointment. She viewed those as personal luxuries for herself that would come at our expense. Mom had one eye on the present and the other on our future.

My mom wasn't like the other moms in the neighborhood. We knew it, and so did all of our friends. They used to call her The Warden! If we weren't at home at a certain time, she would get in her car and cruise around the neighborhood. If she saw any of our friends or anyone who looked like they were our age, she stopped the car, rolled down the window and interrogated them about the last time they had seen us. She then left them with an APB (All Points Bulletin) to tell us to come home if they saw us. And tell us they did!

At the time, Mom's strict discipline was really hard. But just a few years ago, we realized how smart Mom really was all those years. I began to experience an amazing phenomenon: As a teen I thought my mom was old-fashioned, out of touch and clueless, but the older I get, the smarter my mom gets.

A few years ago my brothers and I were sitting down at the Thanksgiving dinner table talking about all our friends in the neighborhood. It started off as a fun conversation, but it didn't end that way. We started talking about Mookie and Tyrone who used to live at the end of the block. They were both high school All-Americans, one as a wrestler and the other as a basketball player. The wrestler was an Olympic hopeful. Today, they're both crack heads. They'll do anything for just one more hit. Their brains are so fried that they walk the streets and don't even know their own names. What a tragedy!

Next door to Mookie and Tyrone was an amazing baseball player named Shaquille. He was a man among boys in Little League. He had a full grown mustache in seventh grade. For real! We all knew that he was going to be the next Sammy Sosa or Ken Griffey, Jr. or Barry Bonds. We fully expected him to sign huge baseball contracts and set all kinds of records one day, but instead he's a drug lord in my city. One of his employees allegedly shot the guy who lived behind us, Kenny, execution-style because he wasn't paying his drug bill on time. Kenny's brother, Boyd, is on parole for pandering—he was running a prostitution ring. Gayle, one of the girls Boyd employed, grew up directly across the street from us, and she died a few years ago from AIDS. Everyone knew Gayle was a strawberry—that's a woman who sells her body for drugs. Even sadder than Gayle was her elderly mom, who roamed the streets at night looking for her daughter, who hadn't been seen in days. After Gayle died, Shaquille bought her home and turned it into a crack house. Shortly after, it became the largest crack house in the county. Now, that's not much of a claim to fame.

Next door to Gayle and her mom was Brady. He was my brother's best friend. Brady made it out. Today, he's a doctor in Dallas, Texas. Unfortunately, his sister, Sherry, wasn't so lucky. In the eighth month of her pregnancy, she overdosed on drugs, killing herself and her baby.

On that Thanksgiving afternoon, we went down the street in our conversation. We went through name after name, face after face, and house after house, and most of the kids we grew up with had either disappeared, been incarcerated, were living on government assistance or had been found dead. We replayed everyone's life. That's when we realized that we were the only complete family to make it out of the neighborhood. There were other people who made it out, but there wasn't a single other house that didn't have at least one sad story like the ones I just told.

The thing is that my brothers and I didn't just make it out of the neighborhood—we made something of ourselves. My brother Kevin is an anesthesiologist and my brother Leon is a lawyer in Southern California. My brother Mark is an engineer who has worked for everyone from Disney to UCLA. He has even helped design sensitive Internet and intranet systems for the U.S. government. (I have this theory that he's really making weapons of mass destruction, but don't tell nobody else that I said that!) My other brother, David, is retired from the military. He served on the U.S.S Peleliu, the ship that brought prisoners over from Afghanistan after September 11. I consider myself the least of my siblings: I graduated from college in less than four years and I'm president and CEO of my own company.

Do you think we made it out of that neighborhood because we were smarter than anybody else? Or because we had more money? Or a special government program? We didn't have any of those things. Sitting at that table on Thanksgiving, we realized that there are three things we had that none of our peers had in the same abundance:

1. We had a God-fearing mother.
2. We had a mother who wasn't afraid to parent.
3. We had a mother who taught a lifestyle of abstinence.

We Had a God-fearing Mother

One of the first memories I can recall is sitting in my brother's lap watching *The Ten Commandments* at Easter. In fact, we were forced to watch that movie every Easter! I remember that as soon as the credits rolled, Mom clicked off the television. (Well, actually, she didn't click it off because we didn't have a remote control. *We* were the remote control.) Mom had one of my brothers turn off the television, and then she started pacing in front of the TV. It was like General Patton was in the room. She told us, "I may not be able to see everything you do or hear everything you say, but God is watching. And every thing you do wrong God is writing in a book. When I get to heaven, I'm going to read that book. And if I don't get you down here, I'm going to get you up there."

As kids, we didn't always understand the concept of an invisible God, but we certainly understood a very visible and audible mom—and whatever we didn't understand, she made very tangible. One of my mom's favorite Scriptures was Proverbs 22:6: "Train a child in the way he should go, and when he is old he will not turn from it."

I remember one time when we were in Pablo's Drugstore deciding what to do with our measly change, collected from under sofa cushions and between car seats, and randomly found on the ground. (An allowance was something the Brady Bunch got. Not us. We had never heard of the word until we saw a rerun of the television show and we asked one another, "What's an allowance?—I don't know.—Maybe Dad knows.—Do you think if we asked him he'd give us one?" My brother was sent to the next room to ask Dad if we could have an allowance. He said we already had one: He allowed us to eat his food, watch his TV and live in his house. And that was a satisfactory answer!)

That day in Pablo's Drugstore, our friends came around the corner when the managers were in the back, and they encouraged us to steal some candy "because no one would know." None of us even thought twice about it. We knew God was watching and He would tell our momma!

Growing up, we only went to church on Easter Sunday. The reason Mom didn't take us to church every Sunday was because she was working full-time as a teacher, getting a masters degree, and raising five kids. The woman was just tired. Also, we learned later in life that our local church had so much chaos, drama and scandal going on that she didn't want us to think that was how God conducted His house. But we kind of figured it out: All of our friends who made it their business to tell us we needed to go to church were also busy blowing weed, flunking out of class and sleeping around. I thought church was where the hypocrites went, and I had enough sense to know that God didn't like it—so I stayed home and worshiped the NFL on Sundays with my family.

The reality is that I had only encountered "make-believers." I wouldn't encounter a *true believer* until much later.

We Had a Mother Who Wasn't Afraid to Parent

Not too long ago, I was walking out of a middle school in Kentucky where I had just given a presentation. In the parking lot, I watched in horror as a girl who was five-foot-nothin' cussed out her momma. Being my mother's daughter, I just couldn't let it go, so I approached the situation and said, "Excuse me, do you eat out of the same dirty mouth you just talked out of?"

Her mother looked at me and said in the most weaselly voice I had ever heard, "She talks to me like that all the time."

I should have double-back slapped that mom. The girl looked at me with her broke-down, Britney Spears wanna-be lookin' self, stomped her foot, put her hands on her hips, rolled her neck at me and said, "You ain't my momma!"

She picked on the wrong sister that day. I told her, "I ain't your dentist either, but I will snatch every tooth out of your head if you talk to me like that!"

The lack of parenting I witness on a regular basis blows me away. I can't believe that woman let her daughter talk to her like that—let alone walk around with a skirt so short it was a belt!

Today "time-out" is a joke. One day one of my brothers cried to my mom and asked why we couldn't get time-outs like the rest of the kids. The phrase "time-out" slapped her ears like a cuss word and she gasped. Then she said, "The only time-outs you're going to get is when I take time out to catch my breath so I can finish whooping your behind. Now go outside and get me a switch." There's nothing worse than having to choose your own weapon of destruction.

The only time-outs Mom ever gave us were times in and out of consciousness, if you know what I mean!

I think one of my mom's favorite Scriptures is "Once they turn a year old you should be able to punch them in the throat and the stomach." No, wait, my bad—that was Bernie Mac. I think Mom likes that Scripture that says "He who spares the rod hates his son, but he who loves him is careful to discipline him" (Prov. 13:24). Well, if that's the case, my mom loved us a whole lot! Spanking is not popular today and in some states it might even be illegal. After a spanking, my mom would hug us and tell us, "I'm your momma and I love you no matter what you think right now, but I'm not trying to win a popularity contest. My job is to be your parent."

Besides the fact that my mom was God-fearing, she was also committed to raising us right. She was not concerned with being our friend. I remember one day my brother Mark looked at her and said, "How come we can't be friends like Gary is with his parents and call you by your first name?"

You can always spot those who have been raised and those who have been trained.

Mom responded, "Boy, there are six billion people on this planet. Anyone of them can be your friend. You only have one momma. You don't like the way I run this house—" She picked up the *Yellow Pages* off the counter and threw them on the floor. "—you don't like the way I run this house? Then you look up another family to go and live with."

As we've grown older, we've all grown closer to Mom. She's become a dear friend and confidant to all of us. But that day when we were still kids, we thought it was hilarious for Mark to even ask.

Mom's philosophy is that children should not be raised—they should be trained. She wasn't interested in being our friend; she was interested in being our mom. She grew up on a farm deep in the South, and she is so country you could spell it with a *K*. She used to say that you *raise* chickens, pigs, horses and cows. Raising provides the minimal requirements of caring for an animal. You give them a safe place and you feed them well. That's how I see a lot of people raising their kids. They have the designer clothes and the latest iPod accessories, are fed a steady diet of MTV, and are given unrestricted access to other forms of media, including the Internet. There's virtually no quality time with their parents. Like farm animals, they're basically left to themselves the majority of the time.

But *training* requires more than just the basics. It takes things like self-sacrifice, service, quality time, affection, discipline and love. Training demonstrates a deeper caring, and it also fosters a sense of mutual appreciation and respect. They used to call it *home training* back in the day. You can always spot those who have been raised and those who have been trained: It shows in how they respect themselves, their peers, and adults, and in their attitude toward life.

We Had a Mother Who Taught a Lifestyle of Abstinence

I've had the opportunity to speak to millions of teens from across the U.S. about abstinence, and you'd be shocked at some of the answers I've gotten when I ask people to define "abstinence." When I first started speaking, I went to a preparatory school in Beverly Hills where they spend a lot of cheese to send their kids to school.

Cheese is the equivalent of cheddar, bling-bling, ice or whatever vernacular kids are using these days for money.

So I asked the crowd, "Can anyone tell me what abstinence is?"

This one chick raised her hand and said, "Um, it's like, um, really, like you know what I'm sayin' . . . it's like a growth that like grows in the back of your neck."

And I said, "No, honey, that's an abscess . . . okay."

Then I got in my car and rolled across to the south side of L.A. to a high school in Compton. As you probably guessed, they don't spend no cheese to send their kids to that broke-down, tore-up school.

So I asked the assembly at Compton, "Can anyone tell me what abstinence is?"

Sista girl raised her hand and said, "Yo, um, it's like this. You know what I'm saying? It's like Mookey and Yoyo told me that Yashika and Camoochi said it was like a bird."

And I said, "No, honey, that's an albatross . . . okay."

People have some crazy definitions for abstinence. But abstinence is not a growth and it is not a bird: *It is saving sex until marriage*. It means waiting until you say "I do"—which means I do you, you do me and we don't do nobody else.

> Abstinence: Waiting until you say "I do"—which means I do you, you do me and we don't do nobody else.

Mom wasn't afraid to talk about abstinence. She was very clear: "You have sex and I will kill you." When I thought of premarital sex, pregnancy and disease were not the first things that came to mind. I feared a major time-out: I might not come back out of consciousness after my mom found out. But the ultimate time-out would be the disappointment I would feel from my mom because she gave me her best and I didn't give it back.

Many people believe abstinence is completely unrealistic—and it is if someone shakes their finger at you, tells you not to do it and then doesn't show you how to live it. My mom demonstrated for us as a single parent what it was to abstain from sex. She didn't have a string of boyfriends sleeping over or living with us. And she didn't just advocate sexual abstinence—she promoted a *lifestyle* of abstinence from all risky behaviors including drugs, alcohol and violence. She knew that if you're not modeling what you're teaching, and then you're teaching something else.

Teaching abstinence isn't shaking your finger and telling someone to "just say no." Teaching abstinence is mastery and demonstration of the arts of self-control, self-discipline and delayed gratification. Many adults are busy telling young people *don't do this* or *don't do that*, which only helps them focus on what *not* to do. Not doing those things becomes its own end. But my parents communicated to us that the things we were to abstain from—including smoking, drinking and promiscuity—were *a means to an end*. The end was a better life, and those things were obstacles that would get in the way.

It wasn't just my mom who taught about abstinence and personal responsibility as a lifestyle.

Every summer when I was growing up, my family would get into our Chevy Suburban (this was before Suburbans were cool) and we would drive across the country from Southern California to see my mom's family in a small town in Alabama. After the Civil War and the slaves were freed, many of my ancestors stayed right there and built the churches, businesses and homes in the entire community. If you met someone on the street and asked them where they came from and they went back far enough in the family tree, chances are good we were related to them. There was a sense of community that I had never experienced before.

During those summer visits, we would sit and listen to stories from aunts and uncles about how things used to be. My paternal grandfather was the pastor of the 16th Street Baptist Church in Birmingham, Alabama, where a bomb went off in the '60s. The story is the basis for Spike Lee's movie *Four Little Girls.* I learned about my uncle, who after retiring from the Air Force, became a professor of engineering at Tuskegee Institute. He designed the carpool system for the Montgom-ery bus boycott during the civil rights movement. I also discovered that when my mom and her sister were college students at Alabama State University, they took a day off from classes to hear the cute new pastor preach at Dexter Avenue Baptist Church. They were disappointed to find out that the pastor's wife, Coretta, was playing the organ. The pastor's name? Martin Luther King, Jr.

I heard stories from one of my younger aunts who used to host Malcolm X and Martin Luther King, Jr. at her boyfriend's parents house. (They are now her in-laws.) Many people know who Rosa Parks was, but she was not the first to be arrested or the last. My aunts and many other college students sat in the front of the bus as a matter of protest, waiting to get arrested.

It was here at the feet of my elders that I began to understand why my parents were the way they were. In the big picture, life and death, success and failure depended on doing what was right and not what was convenient or popular. They disciplined themselves to stand for what was right, even when others mocked, spat at, threatened and abused them. And I thought I had it hard! I realized that I benefited from their discipline and sacrifice.

We grew up hearing about civil rights and we also grew up hearing about personal responsibility. The two are inseparable:

Every right demands responsibility. Growing up, it only made sense that when someone got pregnant, someone got married. If you exercised the right to have sex, then you should step up and be responsible.

Rights and responsibilities apply to every area of our lives, and one summer I discovered how they apply to sex. When I was 11 years old, during my family's annual visit to Alabama, I woke up to discover that my grandfather was nowhere to be found. After a few days, I realized that his disappearance was a daily occurrence. So one afternoon, I decided to wait for him out on the porch. When he finally came back, I asked

Every right demands responsibility.

him, "Granddaddy, where do you go in the mornings?"

"I go to talk to my best friend," he answered.

"Who's that?" I asked.

"Your grandmother," he answered.

Now, my grandmother had been dead for four or five years. But six days a week, excluding Sundays—which was his day of rest—my grandfather would get up while it was still dark and walk down the dirt road with his cane. He loved to make the two-mile journey to his daily destination—our family cemetery—just as the sun was coming up. He would sit in his lounge chair next to her headstone for hours. Then he'd walk two miles back home. He was 90 years old.

"Why do you do this?" I asked.

"Because Ada was my best friend," he said, and started to tear up. "That woman made me feel like I could take over the world. You know, there's nothing I wouldn't have done for her."

As we sat on the porch that morning, my granddaddy told me all kinds of stories about he and my grandmother: how she waited for him to come back from WWI, how she helped spare him from being lynched, and how they got their family through the Great Depression. He also took time to tell me that the first time he ever kissed my grandmother was when the minister said, "You may now kiss the bride."

They were married more than 60 years and raised 12 children together. So it was obvious that after they said "I do" . . . they did.

The last thing my granddaddy said is the thing that I still remember the most from our entire conversation: "You know, I don't know anything about any other woman and I don't want to, because Ada . . . well, she was the stuff."

I remember taking a deep breath in awe. That's what I wanted. I knew from that moment on that afternoon in Alabama that I wanted what my grandparents had. I wanted to be like them and wait until I got married before I had sex. I didn't want to be like other girls in my community, pregnant at 15 years old with stomachs sticking out and sayin', "Where my baby-daddy at? You seen Ray-Ray? Where Ray Ray is?" I didn't want to be an episode of *The Jerry Springer Show*. I wanted "till death do us part."

Now my granddaddy didn't have more than a third-grade education, and he didn't know anything about safe sex. All he knew is that he loved this woman more than life itself, and he was true to her throughout his entire life. That was the vision he gave me at 11 years old that helped me see abstinence as the means to reach the desired end: a deep and lasting love.

> *Vision: A clear picture of what could be, driven by a deep passion that it should be.*—Andy Stanley

What is the vision you have for your life? What will it look like? Is there anyone in your family or neighborhood whose life looks remotely like what you want for yourself? If not, you don't have to repeat their failures. Find someone *somewhere* whose life is worthy of emulation and begin with the end in mind. That means start making decisions today that are conducive to achieving your goal.

What will be the story you'll tell your grandkids one day?

My hope is that you will begin to get a vision for your life and that you'll start to think about your future if you haven't already begun.

Ask Yourself

- Look at the other teens who live in your neighborhood. Where do you see them in 10 years? Where do you see yourself?
- Find someone—maybe a grandparent or elderly person—who waited until they said "I do" to do it. Ask them to tell you their story. Are they glad they waited? If so, why?
- On the timeline provided at left, write some of your dreams and goals. When do you want to graduate? Get married? Have kids? Travel? Buy a house? Retire?
- How do you want your life to be? What does it look like? What kind of life are you going to live? What decisions do you need to make today in order to get there?

CHAPTER 2

The Naked Truth

Once when I was little, my grandmother told me a story. It's a story that has been passed down through my family for generations. She first heard it when she was a small child, and one day, I'm gonna tell it to my children. It's an allegory—a story with a hidden lesson—which are pretty common in the African American community. It goes something like this:

There were two entities. One was called the Truth and the other was called the Lie. Now the Truth and the Lie decided to go skinny-dipping in a nearby pond. It was a hot day, and they knew the swim would cut the heat. So they took off from work and headed toward the local pond. When they got to the pond's bank, they took off all of their clothes and folded them up into two nice little bundles. They both jumped into the water and they started doing the backstroke and the sidestroke. They were having water fights and dunking each other. They were playing games like Marco Polo and having a great afternoon together in the pond.

Eventually the Truth decided it was time to go back to work. He looked around and realized that the Lie has disappeared. So the Truth waded over to the edge of the pond to put his clothes back on and discovered that they had been stolen.

Everything from his Fruit-of-the-Looms to his jock strap—and even the bundle belonging to the Lies—was gone. This brotha was hot! He was not a happy camper.

Truth stormed back into town buck-naked, looking for his clothes. He always knew where the Lie hung out, so he boldly walked up to the steps and began banging on the door of Deception. That's where the Lie usually hung out.

When Lie stepped out on the porch, they erupted into a huge argument. Truth and Lie were so loud that all of the townspeople spilled out into the streets to see what the commotion was all about. And this is what they heard:

Truth confronted the Lie and demanded, "Why did you steal my clothes?"

The Lie said, "I didn't steal your clothes."

"What do you mean you didn't steal my clothes?" Truth asked. "You got my khakis, my FuBu, my Sean John, and my Phat Farm!"

The Lie looked at him and said, "My friend, these have always been my clothes."

The townspeople were confronted with the exact same question that you are confronted with right now, and it is this: Who are you going to believe, a lie in truth's clothing or The Naked Truth?

This is what *The Naked Truth* is all about! We're going to

Who are you going to believe, a lie in truth's clothing or The Naked Truth?

uncover the buck-naked truth about sex. Along the way, we'll undress some lies in truth's clothing that we've all heard and discover The Naked Truth.

Are you ready?

The first step in uncovering The Naked Truth is to know the four steps of good decision making. These steps are not only applicable to the issue of sex, but they also will work for every decision you must make: the issues of drugs, alcohol, peer pressure, college, career and even marriage.

> Step One: Know your options and their consequences.
> Step Two: Make a decision.
> Step Three: Find other people who support your decision.
> Step Four: Take practical steps to achieve your goals.

Step One: Know Your Options and Their Consequences

This is the first step in decision making. Now I know that we live in a culture that divorces consequences from actions—many people think that they can do what they want and nothing will happen to them, because somebody else will clean up their mess. But guess what? That's not The Naked Truth.

Nobody's born a loser, but everybody's born a chooser. Either you're going to benefit or you're going to suffer from every decision you make in this lifetime. You may not see the consequences of your actions by the end of the day, the end of the week, the end of the semester, the time you graduate or even in five or ten years . . . but rest assured: What goes around comes around, and you will reap what you sow.

Step Two: Make a Decision

This is the second step in the decision-making process. The act of making a decision means that you have a timeline in mind to reach your goals, that you've drawn the boundaries that will help you get there, and that you've planned to regularly reassess your progress, all in order to obtain your goals.

Step Three: Find Other People Who Support Your Decision

You just can't do it on your own. Once you make a decision, you need people in your life who have your back. You've got to have people who will not just support you but also help you stay committed to your decision. The company you keep says a whole lot about just how much you want to reach your goal.

I've had a lot of great friends in my life, but one of the best was my college roommate. We had a lot in common when it came to our goals and our values—not just for school but in our relationships, too. We didn't do that thing where one person puts a handkerchief outside the door to tell the other person "Me and my boyfriend are getting busy, so don't come in." We didn't do that. Instead, we held each other accountable to our commitment. Whenever there were issues and we were struggling with something—whether it was a guy or whatever—we told each other. We were open about it. And you know what? We stayed roommates for all four years of college. To this day, we're still friends. Finding other people who will support your decisions is very important.

Step Four: Take Practical Steps to Achieve Your Goals.

If you fail to plan, you plan to fail. This applies to every single area of your life. If you set a goal, you're not just going to wake up one day and find that it's magically happened. It's going to take planning, work and follow-through. For instance, once I made the decision to make abstinence a lifestyle, I had to do

If you fail to plan, you plan to fail.

something about it. Right after I graduated from college, I went out and bought a purity ring. It was a promise ring that represented my commitment to wait to have sex until I got married.

The ring would go everywhere I went, into every situation and every relationship. I still have that ring, and I met that goal by waiting until I said "I do" to do it.

The Marshmallow Test

A number of years back, Stanford University conducted an interesting study. They took a group of kids around five years old from a wide variety of socio-economic and racial backgrounds, and then gave them a marshmallow.

The researcher then told the kids, "I've given you one marshmallow, and now I'm going to leave. I'll be gone for 20 minutes, and if you can wait until I get back to eat the marshmallow, I'll give you two more."

They captured the kids' behavior on camera and I watched it on *Oprah* a while back. (You know if it's on *Oprah,* it must be true.) Anyway, they showed how these kids responded. Some of them burst into tears because they couldn't get their way—they wanted to eat their one marshmallow *right now* and also get two more. It was too much pressure. There were others who—as soon as the researcher left—licked the bottom of their marshmallows and then stuck them back on the plate. A few other kids just sat there and tormented themselves, staring at their marshmallow with mouths watering. And then there were the kids who just couldn't wait. They picked at their marshmallows and nibbled off little pieces. A few kids even tried to hollow out their marshmallows, hoping the researcher wouldn't notice! And finally, there was a small number of kids who occupied themselves with a toy or a book, or by looking out the window. They totally forgot the marshmallow was in the room.

When the researcher came back, she rewarded each of the kids. Those who had waited got more marshmallows, while the ones who didn't wait didn't get any more.

But that wasn't the end of the experiment! The researchers tracked down the exact same kids 10 years later. They discovered that the kids who had the ability to wait scored an average of more than 200 points higher on their SATs. The kids who waited for their rewards had lower occurrences of juvenile delinquency, drug abuse, alcohol abuse and other risky behaviors.

What they found out is that some of the kids had developed a high emotional quotient. It's like an emotional IQ, and those who have a high emotional IQ have figured out *self-mastery*. In other words, those who have the ability to exercise self-control, self-discipline and delayed gratification are the ones who have mastered the art of achieving success, because they know how to work for it and they know how to wait for it.[1]

You may be wondering, *What's my emotional IQ?* I can't tell you. But I can tell you this: No matter what your emotional IQ is today, it can be higher tomorrow. You see, while a regular IQ doesn't usually change over a lifetime, your emotional quotient can change at any time.

It doesn't matter what you did yesterday; it matters what you're going to do today. Your future and your ability to achieve sustained success in life are based on your ability to master the skills of self-control, self-discipline and delayed gratification.

You cannot achieve sustained success in life unless you have mastered these three skills. I say *sustained success* because our culture often tells us that true success, like sex, should come quick, fast and in a hurry. The reality is that true success—sustained success and a great sex life—doesn't come in an instant. It comes with endurance.

Abstinence is mastering the art of self-control, self-discipline and delayed gratification. It's not just something you do or don't do: It's a lifestyle. So let's talk about the three components of that lifestyle.

The Three Components of the Abstinent Lifestyle

1. Self-control
2. Self-discipline
3. Delayed gratification

The first component of an abstinent lifestyle is *self-control*. Self-control is *not doing something* you want to do when you want to do it. Like eating. Have you seen the Lays ad that says, "You can't just eat one"? Well, self-control says, "Yes, I *can* eat just one. In fact, I can take it to the next level and not eat any at all if I don't want to! Just watch me!"

Now it's not just food where we must exercise self-control. We can learn to do it in many areas of our lives, including what comes out of our mouths. Yeah, some people can't stop running their mouths and talking all the time . . . and it gets them in trouble. Self-control knows when to speak up and when to stay silent.

Self-control is not doing something you want to do when you want to do it.

The second component of an abstinent lifestyle is *self-discipline*. It's a little bit different than self-control. Self-discipline is doing something you don't want to do when you don't want to do it. Like taking out the trash. No one really likes taking out the trash, and if everybody refuses to do it, eventually you'll see it piling up and climbing the walls. That's when self-discipline kicks in. You don't want to take out the trash, but you do it because you know that there is a future reward: Your parents will stop nagging you.

Or take something simple like homework. I never liked homework, but I did it so that I wouldn't have to take the same class twice. I wanted to get out of high school. I wanted to go to college. And I didn't want my momma bugging me. So I forced myself to do something that I really didn't feel like doing, because I realized there was a future reward.

The third component of the abstinent lifestyle is *delayed*

Self-discipline is doing something you don't want to do when you don't want to do it.

gratification. Delayed gratification is the consistent practice of both self-control and self-discipline, because you realize there is a future reward if you practice those skills on a regular basis. In fact, delayed gratification recognizes that the future reward is far greater than the fleeting thrill of instant gratification.

It wasn't that long ago that I was a cheerleader. As a matter of fact, I was an All-American. After graduation, I modeled for some of the largest athletic apparel companies, like Nike and Reebok, and I also danced professionally. It was my job to stay in shape. (Obviously, that was a couple Krispy Kremes ago.) Basically, my job was to work out every day in order to get a job. Some of my former workout partners are people whose names you'd recognize. They play in the NFL and the NBA. We got up every morning at 4:30 A.M. and ran two miles, then rode our bikes for 10 miles. I'd come home and eat breakfast—which was usually scrambled egg whites and broccoli—and then read and pray for an hour before going back to the gym to lift weights. After weight training, I went to the dance studio to train for three more hours.

Do you know how much discipline it takes to be a model or dancer? Do you know how much discipline it takes to be a professional athlete? It takes a lot. It requires you to discipline *everything*, from your eating habits to your exercise habits to your sleeping habits.

It's easy to give props to discipline in athletics or even academics, but it's sad that we don't applaud it in our personal lives. When I danced professionally, I was not a video ho-fessional. I didn't do the bump 'n' grind, because I made a decision that I would never take a job that would require me to compromise my beliefs or to prostitute myself. As a matter of fact, I turned down more jobs than I ever worked because I figured that if I wouldn't want my mom to turn on the TV and see it, I shouldn't be doing it.

Even if you're not going to be in the NBA or NFL or on the cover of magazines, you can still be disciplined and motivated in your personal life. You may think there's nothing to get jazzed about, but that just means that you're focusing on the wrong thing. Don't focus on the discipline. Find a vision or a goal that's worthy enough of undivided attention, and it will motivate you to work toward that goal.

Even if you still can't name your specific goal or vision, there are some things in life that almost everyone on the planet is striving for: a long, healthy, prosperous life; a sense of purpose and well being; and of course, a happy sex life.

Which of the following do you want? Check all that apply:

- ❑ Long life
- ❑ Health
- ❑ Prosperity (a.k.a. "bling-bling")
- ❑ Sense of purpose
- ❑ Happy sex life

If you're going to achieve any of the things on the list, then you have to begin with the end in mind. You have to begin making decisions today that will lead you toward your goal tomorrow. Success in these areas and others requires self-control, self-discipline and delayed gratification.

The entry on the checklist that probably caught your attention (and mine!) is a happy sex life. Who doesn't want that? The fact is, the happiest sex lives are found among those who wait until marriage to have sex, which requires self-control, self-discipline and delayed gratification. But just like the kids with the marshmallows, those who wait are richly rewarded.

You have to begin with the end in mind.

How do I know? Because I waited, and believe me, it is oh-so-true! When I talk about abstinence or waiting to have sex, it's not because I think sex is bad or sex is evil—just the opposite. Sex is a very, very good gift from God. Thank You, Lord!

Ask Yourself

- Make a list of your goals. Think big!
- Now make a list of the people supporting you as you reach those goals. Do you have any friends who are holding you back from reaching your goals?
- Now make a list of the steps you need to take to meet those goals. Save your list and begin checking off those steps as you get closer to meeting your goals.
- If you were taking the marshmallow test, what would you do with your marshmallow?
- What are some areas in your life where you can begin practicing delayed gratification?

CHAPTER 3

It Can't Happen to Me

My friend Barb Wise says that she had been taught not to have sex until marriage, but she was never given any of the skills on how to set boundaries.

"I didn't know how to say no," she says. "I had no skills, so when I went to college, I started drinking and each time I would push boundaries farther and farther. Afterward, I'd try to minimize it and tell myself that at least I wasn't as bad as some of the girls. I'd actually try to bargain with God and tell Him that the sexual contact I was having wasn't technically intercourse and that the desires I was feeling were actually God's fault—since He had made me that way."

The lines kept getting pushed farther and farther until one night, when she was 19, an older man invited her over to his house. Everything in her being told her not to go, but she went anyway and ended up having sex with him.

"Afterward, I was devastated," she says.

She quickly ended the relationship and began looking for another boyfriend. She found herself dating guy after guy. As soon as the relationship would go bad, she would pick out the next guy and go sexually as far as he wanted to go.

She dated dozens and dozens of guys. Eventually, she realized the vicious cycle that she was caught in. She knew that she had to make being in a good, healthy relationship with God and a guy her goal.

At 27, she met Rick at a Christian singles' group. He casually mentioned that he was a virgin, and Barb felt compelled to tell him about her past. He said that there might be some consequences to her actions, and they'd deal with them if they ever came up.

Barb thought he was naïve. How could there be any consequences? Everything would be fine, but just to make sure she decided to get tested. That's when she found out that she was HIV-positive.

When it comes to sex, you have two options, and both of them have consequences:

- Option #1: Decide that you will start having sex and/or continue having sex outside of marriage.

- Option #2: Decide that you will wait for marriage to have sex.

Consequences for Option #1

Okay, so you decide that you will start or continue to bang everything that walks on two legs. Can you think of any consequences? Consider the following list. Put a check by all that apply:

- ❑ Pregnancy
- ❑ Sexually Transmitted Diseases (STDs)
- ❑ Heartbreak
- ❑ Emotional baggage
- ❑ Loss of focus

- ❑ Loss of dreams and goals
- ❑ Bad reputation

The Naked Truth is that *all* of these apply, and more! There are not only physical, psychological, emotional, relational and social consequences of having sex out of marriage, but there are also economic and legal consequences.

> ***DID YOU KNOW?*** Social science data show that teens who abstain from sex do substantially better on a wide range of outcomes. For example, teens who abstain from sex are less likely to be depressed and attempt suicide, to experience STDs, to have children out of wedlock and to live in poverty and welfare dependence as adults.[1]

Consequences for Option #2

Consider the following list. Put a check by all that apply:

- ❑ Avoid pregnancy
- ❑ Avoid STDs
- ❑ Less heartbreak
- ❑ Less emotional baggage
- ❑ Keeping your focus
- ❑ Keeping your dreams and goals alive
- ❑ Keeping a good reputation
- ❑ Relationships built without interference from sex

The Naked Truth is that *all* of these apply, and more! There are physical, psychological, emotional, relational and social consequences of waiting until marriage to have sex, and they're all for your benefit!

DID YOU KNOW? Those who practice abstinence are more likely to have stable and enduring marriages as adults.[2]

If you've opted for Option No. 1 in the past, then hopefully you'll want to make a decision for Option No. 2 for the future. The Naked Truth is that even if you have had sex in the past, you can still choose abstinence as a lifestyle. It's something we call secondary virginity, and it's a commitment to wait to have sex from this day forward until marriage. While you can never get your virginity back physically, you can regain it emotionally, psychologically, spiritually and relationally.

Secondary virginity is a commitment to wait to have sex from this day forward until marriage.

Sexually Transmitted Diseases

Let's get down to one of the big consequences for choosing to have sex before marriage: sexually transmitted diseases (STDs). It's easy to think that it won't happen to you. But just like Barb, the reality is that it can, and odds are that it will! You see, in our grandparents' day, there were only two major STDs that people had to worry about: syphilis and gonorrhea. If you contracted either one, all you had to do was get a big shot of penicillin in the butt and they went away. Today, however, there are more than 25 different categories of STDs. Mind you, when I say categories, I mean that if you get herpes, the question is what strain of herpes did you get? There's not just one or two or three or even four strains of herpes—there are eight different strains! And you can get infected with one or two or three or a combination of all eight strains at the same time.

Now you may not think herpes is any big thing. We've all seen the Valtrex commercial—you know the one—where the beautiful people are shot in black and white, kayaking down a river or running down the beach in slow motion while holding hands. The girl comments that having a herpes outbreak is such a hassle . . . she doesn't have time to deal with the inconvenience of all the complicated medications. "And that's why there's Valtrex," she says, right before the announcer (who raps faster than Tongue Twista) jumps in to mumble about the side effects, which may include: abdominal pain, aggressive behavior, agitation, allergic reactions, confusion, depression, diarrhea, dizziness, facial swelling, hallucinations, headache, high blood pressure, joint pain, mania, menstrual problems, nausea, rapid heartbeat, rash and vomiting.

Girlfriend shoulda thought twice about the hassle or inconvenience before she laid down and had sex!

DID YOU KNOW? When compared to sexually active teens, teens who abstain from sex during high school years (e.g., at least until age 18) are:

- less likely to be depressed and to attempt suicide
- less likely to experience STDs
- less likely to have children out of wedlock
- less likely to live in poverty and welfare dependence as adults
- more likely to have stable and enduring marriages as adults
- 60 percent less likely to be expelled from school
- 50 percent less likely to drop out of high school
- almost twice as likely to graduate from college[3]

Here's what Valtrex won't tell you: You need different medicines based on which strains of herpes you get infected with. If you have more than one, you'll need a different medicine for each strain. Herpes isn't just a hassle—it can also be painful and expensive buying all those medicines.

The same is true with hepatitis. If someone says they got hepatitis from having sex, the next question is, *What kind did you get?* There are different strains of hepatitis: A, B, C, D and G strains. (Not G-*string*, mind you . . . G *strain*.) That's five different types of hepatitis, and not all of them have cures.

If you count up all the various strains in all the different categories, there are countless different sexually transmitted diseases waiting for you out there. Sex is not like it used to be! Our grandparents had to worry about two STDs; we have to worry about hundreds! Most of them are painful and embarrassing, and many are hard to pronounce, like human papillomavirus (also known as genital warts). There's pelvic inflammatory disease, Chlamydia and crabs (also known as pubic lice). There's hepatitis B, trichomoniasis and herpes, a graduation gift that keeps on giving. Once you got it, it's got you—and it ain't goin' nowhere, if you know what I mean.

There are three types of STDs that you can get: a virus, a bacteria and a bacterial virus.

A virus means that you will have it for the rest of your life. You can't get rid of it. Viruses usually have the letter *V* in them, like in human papillomavirus (HPV) or human immunodeficiency virus (HIV). Hepatitis B and herpes are also viruses. Sometimes people don't show any signs that they're infected with a virus, and it may take years for symptoms like lesions or sores to show.

The good news is, you can get rid of bacteria and bacterial viruses with the right medication. But you have to know you have them before you can get rid of them.

V vs. B: Virus or Bacteria?

Put a "V" next to every STD that's a virus and a "B" next to every STD that's a bacteria:

__Herpes
__Syphilis
__Gonorrhea
__Genital Warts
__Hepatitis
__HIV/AIDS

You may think that with all the new medicines, getting an STD is no big deal. But it will change your life! Did you know that if a mother has herpes and she has an outbreak during birth, there is a significant chance that her baby will die? (That's why mothers who have active herpes have to get a C-section rather than deliver naturally–it's the only way to keep the baby safe.)

If a mother has HIV or AIDS, there's a good chance that her baby will be born with the disease. And even if it's not, the mom cannot breastfeed the baby, because AIDS is transmitted from mother to child through breast milk.

Not all STDs will affect your children–some will prevent you from having any. Some diseases will leave you sterile and you'll never be able to have kids. Some of them are incurable, meaning you'll have them for the rest of your life.

And some of them are deadly.

Of all the different sexually transmitted diseases, what's the one that gets the most attention? AIDS. What happens when you get AIDS, people? Barring a miracle or an array of very expensive medication, you die. What you may not know is that AIDS is not the only STD that can kill you. We'll talk more about that later.

First, let's take The Naked Truth Quiz. In other words, let's find out what you *really* know about STDs:

Answers: Herpes=Virus; Genital Warts=Virus; Syphilis=Bacteria; Hepatitis=Virus; Gonorrhea=Bacteria; HIV/AIDS=Virus.

THE NAKED TRUTH Quiz

1. 42,000 people get a sexually transmitted disease in the U.S.
   A) every day.
   B) every month.
   C) every year.
   D) every decade.

2. Two-thirds of the people who get an STD this year will be
   A) 25 years old or younger.
   B) 25 to 40 years old.
   C) 40 to 55 years old.
   D) 55 years old or older.

3. What percentage of sexually active single adults have at least one STD?
   A) 25%
   B) 50%
   C) 75%
   D) 100%

4. One in _____ Americans over the age of 12 has herpes.
   A) 100
   B) 50
   C) 25
   D) 5

5. By the time they graduate from high school, one in ____ sexually active teens has an STD.
   A) 100
   B) 50
   C) 25
   D) 4

6. Nearly __________ teenage girls get pregnant every year in the U.S.
   A) 100,000
   B) 500,000
   C) 800,000
   D) 1 million

Answer 1

A. The Naked Truth is that more than 42,000 people get a sexually transmitted disease in the U.S. *every day*.[4] Now let's put this in perspective. About 1,500 people die every day from cancer in America. And 2,600 or so die every day from some kind of heart-related illness, like stroke or heart attack. How many get an STD every day? More than 50,000. How many got one yesterday? More than 50,000. How many are going to get one today? More than 50,000. How many are going to get one tomorrow? More than 50,000. How many will get one the day after tomorrow? More than 50,000. And if we were to continue for 365 days, we'd be talking about more than 19 million people contracting an STD in America *every year*. The population of the U.S.A. is only 300 million.

Answer 2

A. The Naked Truth is that two-thirds of the people who get an STD this year will be 25 years old and younger. Just a few years ago, 19 million Americans contracted an STD in one single year, and even then, two-thirds of those infected were college-age students and younger.[5]

Answer 3

B. The Naked Truth is that one-half (50%) of all sexually active single adults have, or will have, at least one STD. Most are walking around with one right now and don't even know it. That means that if you throw this book aside and you decide you're going to start or continue having sex outside of marriage—protected or unprotected—there's a greater than 50/50 chance that you will contract at least one STD in your lifetime.[6]

Answer 4

D. The Naked Truth is that one in five Americans over the age of 12 has herpes.[7]

Answer 5

D. The Naked Truth is that one in four sexually active teens has an STD by the time they graduate from high school.[8] For you girls, that means that one out of four sexually active guys walking around your school—the one who's about to graduate, that you think is so fine—already has an STD.

Answer 6

C. The Naked Truth is that 800,000 teenage girls get pregnant every year in the U.S. The vast majority of those girls weren't planning on getting pregnant, and they didn't think it could happen to them.[9]

So how did you do on The Naked Truth Quiz?

1-2 Correct:	"Get your head together!""
3-5 Correct:	"Awright."
6 Correct:	"You go!"

Sexually transmitted diseases aren't something that happen to other people. They are the consequences of somebody's actions, and they can happen to you. The odds are that if you choose to do it before you get married, you may as well stop asking if you're going to get an STD and start asking which one you're going to catch.

The Naked Truth is that a lot of people who have an STD don't even know they have one. If you have been sexually active, how do you know if you have an STD? By getting tested. One of the places you can go is a Crisis Pregnancy Center, many of which offer testing for STDs. Also, there are free clinics in many communities where you can go in and get tested anonymously. They also do testing at some blood drives, which are often held at schools or in your local community.

It Can't Happen To Me

In case you couldn't tell, we're in a national state of emergency. Unless you've been living in a cave with Osama Bin Laden for the last several years, you know we've been in a state of emergency since September 11. But The Naked Truth is that we were in one long before September 11, and it wasn't because of terrorism. As a matter of fact, before President Clinton left office, he declared a national state of emergency when the Centers for Disease Control notified him that the common cold is no longer the most commonly reported virus. It is now sexually transmitted diseases, and the majority of these are contracted by teenagers and young adults.

STDs don't just inconvenience you. They don't only cost you in terms of medical bills and discomfort and embarrassment. They can also kill you.

You might think that STDs and pregnancies only happen to trailer trash, ghetto hood rats, and barrio hos, but the Naked Truth is that they can happen to anyone. "It can't happen to me" is a lie in truth's clothing. If the statistics we just looked at mean anything, STDs and teenage pregnancy happen to a lot of people—probably someone you already know.

People don't want to tell you The Naked Truth, but the reality is that these are just the physical consequences. We haven't started talking about the emotional consequences of having your heart broken by somebody you really cared about and now they're telling all their friends that you didn't mean anything to them. We haven't talked about the psychological drama of your ex giving some of your friends the "benefits" you used to get. We haven't talked about some of the other legal and financial stuff that come with not living an abstinent lifestyle. Guys, what about the financial consequences of having your paycheck garnished every month for the next 18 years to a girl you don't even like anymore so that she can provide for your baby? I'm tellin' you this because most people believe the lie in truth's clothing that actions have no consequences.

> Like my guy friend told me: "Don't keep him, release him." I took his advice, but a year later he was having issues with his about-to-be fiancée, so I told him: "Don't chase her, replace her."

I was speaking at a preparatory school—the one where the girl said that "Abstinence is, like, um, a growth in the back of your, like, neck"—and a girlfriend of Abscess Girl came up after my talk and engaged me in a conversation. It took forever for her to explain her situation because every other word was "um, like" and "you know what I'm saying?" With Ms. Abscess standin' by, she fidgeted around, saying, "I don't know what happened," as she twirled her bleached-out permed locks. "It's like I woke up one morning and I was pregnant."

Fifty percent of teen pregnancies are fathered by men over the age of 20.

Yeah, right! Like she don't know how that happened. I couldn't let this teaching opportunity pass by so I pulled her aside and slowly explained in my best big-sista voice: "Girl-friend, I don't know if anyone has ever told you this or not but . . . if you don't have sex, you won't get pregnant." Everybody, including her, knew *exactly* what happened, but I can't tell you how many times I hear this lie in truth's clothing.

As you found out in The Naked Truth Quiz, 800,000 teenage girls get pregnant each year in the U.S. This may be a surprise to you, but half of them are fathered by men over the age of 20. In fact, males aged 20 years or older father five times as many births among middle school-aged girls as middle school-aged boys.[10]

This tells me something not only about the girls but also about the guys. Take note: Those guys hanging out after school, down the street in the car, waiting for you to get out of school—they're not someone's older brother! Why do you think these guys, 20 years *and older*, are hanging out at local high schools and middle schools? Maybe you truly believe its because of all the lies—I mean, *lines*—he's told you, like "You're special . . . you're not like all the other girls." Let me interpret this for you:

He Says	He Means
"You're special."	"You're on *today's* special . . . *fresh meat*!"
"You're not like all the other girls."	"When I get in *your* panties, you'll be like the other girls I've been with."

The reason he's hanging out with you is because the girls his own age won't give him the time of day. He's a loser. That's right, I said it and I'll say it again: loser! What in the world does a grown man have in common with a middle school student? And, ladies, your ability to relate to an adult male in this situation is not a reflection on *your* maturity, but a reflection of *his* lack thereof. (And by the way, chances are he's picking you up in his momma's car, 'cause that's who he lives with. Just thought you ought to know.)

Should I continue with the list of reasons that older guys try to pick up on girls your age? I think so, because there are a few of you who will continue to be in denial. (Most of you will take this to heart as a heads up or confirmation of what you already know to be true.) I have had many conversations with reformed and not-so-reformed players, and when it comes down to it, they say they prey on "fresh meat" because of a few basic things.

***Four out of 10 teenage girls are infected with at least one STD the first time they have sex.*[11]**

First, they're looking for a girl with low self-esteem—particularly those with no male figures in their life to encourage or protect them, such as a father and big brothers.

Second, they figure that when a girl is young, she hasn't had a lot of sexual experience (and even if you lie and say you have, they can tell). They're banking on the idea that if a girl is young, she's probably a virgin, and it will be easier to convince her to have sex. They think young girls are easy. I had one guy tell me, "They don't know nothin', and they believe whatever I tell them. After we've been having sex, they think no other guy will ever want them and they'd be better off staying with me. Guess what? They stay and do what I tell them. After a while you get tired of them and find another 'chicken head' or 'sweetie.' You got to cut 'em loose, and that's when they be all crying and stuff. But you know, a brotha's got to move on!"

Third, they think if you haven't been around the block, then you won't have a sexually transmitted disease. I had another guy tell me that it was his "personal mission" to rid his community of virgins. "Yeah, I have an STD," he said. "These high school girls are so stupid, all you have to do is let them talk, talk, talk. Just pretend like you're really interested and after a while she'll tell you exactly what you need to know so then you can tell her exactly what she wants to hear. And then, BAM! She'll give it up, dude, fo' real, and I don't even have to worry about getting a disease because she was a virgin! Once I had this junior high school chick, who was a virgin."

"You were in junior high?" I asked.

He laughed and looked sideways at me. "No, this was last year."

The guy was 23.

"She asked me to wear protection, which I never wear unless it's to gain their trust. I did. Of course, I knew she'd stop asking for it, because we were 'in love'—yeah right! When she told me her parents found out about the condoms and that she was having sex, I thought I'd better seek protection for myself, since she was a minor. I don't know if she found out that I left her a little somethin' somethin', but if she ever does, I know she'll never tell anyone it was me."

This guy is only saying what I've heard a lot of guys say: "If you get them young, chances are you won't get an STD." But that doesn't mean that *you* won't get one, girls. As a matter of fact, four out of ten teenage girls are infected with at least one STD the first time they have sex. Just thought you might want to know that.

Now, fellas, if half of teen pregnancies are fathered by men over the age of 20, this tells me something about some of you, too.

I love to people-watch, and before I speak before a crowd, I usually stand off to the side, lean back "in the cut" and observe people strolling in. My favorites are the guys who pimp walk confidently into the room as if they are the only ones in attendance, as if they know they are secretly being filmed by a reality TV show. You know the ones: They nod with their chin as they pass their fans and admirers, and might even speak a friendly "wassup?" They wink at a couple of the honeys before they sit and then slowly slide down into their seat before leaning over to the side.

I can see and hear them even now. They're the ones who make wise remarks while I'm talking, but I usually ignore them—I have been known to reduce grown men to tears, and I wouldn't want to emotionally scar them for life. Instead, I give them the I-am-not-the-sista-you-want-to-mess-with look and continue on.

You know these guys. They try to intimidate you in the locker room and hallways, but you give "the nod" with the chin back so that they don't "peep you out." They're the guys who give other dudes a hard time because they're virgins and they brag often about their own sexual exploits.

Well, fellas, rest assured: These guys are frontin' . . . they're lying . . . they ain't getting none. The numbers don't lie. They need to get on home an' bust some suds, 'cause the only exploits they've had is the last episode of *Sponge Bob*.

I talk to a half a million kids every single year, and I take a poll and ask the same question of every group. Now I'm going to ask you:

When is the most appropriate occasion to have sex for the first time?

I give my audience two options, and they cheer for the one they like best:

(A) The most appropriate occasion to have sex for the first time is marriage.
(B) The most appropriate occasion is on prom night with a condom.

Of course, the second answer is the one that gets the loudest response. Then I respond, "You think that prom night is the best time?"

Now there are more screams and whistles. And that's when I drop it: "I knew you'd say that, which is the reason more stupid girls get pregnant on prom night than any other night of the year." (Silence.) "How do I know? Because I can count to nine, boys and girls. Count nine months after prom, and you'll see the influx of high school girls in hospital maternity wards around the country. Don't let that be you."

> *I'm into having sex, I ain't into making love, so come give me a hug if you into getting' rubbed . . .* —50 Cent, *"In Da Club"*[12]

On prom night, you won't just find girls getting pregnant and STDS, you'll also find a lot of drunk driving going on. And that's not a good idea.

The abstinent lifestyle is not just abstinence from sex. It includes abstinence from alcohol and drugs as well. Scholars, there's a reason they're called "mind-altering substances" . . . because you'll find yourself doing things you wouldn't ordinarily do with people you wouldn't ordinarily be seen with. There is profound truth in the saying "The more you drink, the better looking certain people get." This phenomenon is often referred to as *beer goggling.*

There are people who don't intend to drink or leave a party stoned. You may be one of them, but you should plan to bring your own punch because you may not know what somebody put in it. In my town, there were a bunch of women who went to a few parties, only to wake up the following morning and discover they had been assaulted. They couldn't remember a thing. We later found out that the perpetrator was the DJ at my girlfriend's wedding!

The bottom line is that drugs and alcohol impair your ability to make wise decisions about what you do with your body and who you do it with, whether you get in the front seat for a ride or the backseat for a different kind of ride. If you want to live an abstinent lifestyle, then alcohol and drugs are not an option.

Remember, focusing on *not* having sex, *not* taking drugs and *not* drinking alcohol is *not* the core of the abstinent lifestyle. Not doing those things is the means to an end. It is the elimination of things that will prevent or impair your ability to fulfill your potential.

My friend Donald Bell (often referred to as "The Urban Dr. Phil") once said, "Potential means not yet or maybe never." All of us have unfulfilled potential. So begin with the end in mind and start fulfilling yours today!

sow a thought, reap an act, sow an act, reap a habit
sow a habit, reap a lifestyle, sow a lifestyle, reap a character
sow a character, reap a destiny
—James Allen, English author

Ask Yourself

- Why do you think people don't talk about STDs?
- Why do you think so many people think that STDs can't happen to them? What would you say is The Naked Truth about STDs?
- Think of someone you know who is sexually active. What are the odds that person has an STD?
- Why is it important to avoid alcohol and drugs as part of the abstinent lifestyle?

CHAPTER 4

America's Most Unwanted

The American population is being silently terrorized by gangs of the most undesirable sexually transmitted diseases ever known. This criminal element assaults millions of unsuspecting victims each year with painful, damaging and sometimes deadly force. Most victims are unknowing accomplices to their own demise and the infection of others. If you or someone you know has engaged in sex outside of a mutually monogamous domestic lifetime partnership (a.k.a. marriage), it's possible that you or the person you know may have already been assaulted and become unsuspecting accomplices to these assailants.

The criminals at large are part of two powerful mob families—La Familia Bacterial and La Familia Viral—as well as a host of lesser gangs and cell groups that silently commit violent offenses against citizens, often targeting the younger population. You could be a victim of . . . America's Most Unwanted.

The Usual Suspects

La Familia Bacterial (Bacterial STDs)

Medea	a.k.a.	Chlamydia
Rhea	a.k.a.	Gonorrhea
Phyllis	a.k.a.	Syphilis
P-Deasy	a.k.a.	PID (Pelvic Inflammatory Disease)

La Familia Viral (Viral STDs)

G-Dub	a.k.a.	Human Papillomavirus (HPV)
Herp	a.k.a.	Herpes
Notorious HIV	a.k.a.	HIV/AIDS

Gangs and Cell Groups

The Crabs	a.k.a.	Pubic Lice
Trixie	a.k.a.	Trichomoniasis

America's Most Unwanted

Profile: Phyllis, a.k.a. Syphilis

The Accused: Phyllis, a.k.a. Syphilis**.** A popular member of the Bacterial Family, she has often been called "the great imitator" since evidence left at the scene of the crime is often indistinguishable from that of other diseases. (Other known aliases: "the clap.")

Victims: Anyone engaged in any kind of sexual activity is fair game to Phyllis. Her victims are primarily 20 to 39 years of age, and men are preferred: one-and-a-half times more men than women fall prey. Newborns also become her victim, as a mother can pass Phyllis along to her fetus during pregnancy, increasing the risk of a stillbirth or a baby that dies soon after delivery. Untreated babies may become developmentally delayed, have seizures or die. The CDC (Center for Disease Control) estimates that Phyllis assaults 70,000 new victims annually. Because her crime goes undetected, officials reported only 35,600 cases in 1999. Without knowing it, nearly 35,000 of her victims became accomplices in expanding her crime network across America.

Crime Scene: Genitals and genital area, mouth, anus.

Modus Operandi: Genital contact, oral sex and anal sex. Phyllis carries out her operations through skin-to-skin contact with open sores. She has been known to evade condom security when lesions or warts remain exposed.

Evidence: Often spotted as a single painless sore called a chancre (pronounced "SHANK-er") between 10 and 90 days after contact. On average, the sore will appear within 21 days. Although Phyllis's sores sometimes disappear without treatment, other evidence of her crime may appear several weeks to six months after her initial assault. Other evidence includes a rash, genital lesions, sores on the mouth, throat or cervix, patchy loss of hair, general sense of ill health (making symptoms indistinguishable from other diseases). When the evidence goes undetected or unreported, the victim can become one of Phyllis's many unsuspecting accomplices, spreading the disease if he or she continues to engage in sexual activity. Genital sores (chancres) caused by

---

Profile continued on next page.

syphilis make it easier to transmit and acquire Notorious HIV.

The Crime: The offense and consequences of undetected Phyllis can remain in the body of her victims and progress in stages that can damage internal organs—including the brain, heart, nerves (can lead to paralysis), eyes (can lead to blindness), blood vessels, liver, bones and joints—and can eventually lead to death (preceded by dementia).

Investigation: Blood test administered by a crime scene investigator (physician)

Apprehension: Since she is part of the Bacterial Family, Phyllis can be fully apprehended (cured). However, victims should seek immediate medical treatment when evidence has been found. There are no home remedies or over-the-counter drugs that will cure syphilis. Victims may be treated by injection with penicillin or other antibiotics to kill the bacteria and prevent further damage, but it will not repair damage already done.

Prevention: See Self-Defense Manual.

Sources

American Social Health Association. "Syphilis Fast Facts." http://www.ashastd.org/learn/learn_syphilis_facts.cfm.
Centers for Disease Control and Prevention. "Sexually Transmitted Diseases: Syphilis." http://www.cdc.gov/std/syphilis/default.htm.
Cox, M., ed., *Questions Kids Ask About Sex*. Grand Rapids, MI: Baker Book House, 2005.
National Coalition of STD Directors. "Quick Facts: Syphilis." http://www.ncsddc.org/syphilis.htm.
Swartz, M. N., B. P. Healey and D. M. Musher. "Late Syphilis," cited in Holmes, et al., eds. *Sexually Transmitted Diseases*. New York: McGraw Hill, 1999, pp. 487-509.

America's Most Unwanted

Profile: Notorious HIV, a.k.a. HIV/AIDS

The Accused: Notorious HIV, a.k.a. HIV/AIDS. Perhaps the most famous member of the Viral Family, human immunodeficiency virus invades the immune system of the body and destroys it over time, reducing a person's ability to fight off infections and diseases. When this happens, HIV introduces his partner in crime: AIDS (Acquired Immune Deficiency Syndrome). Notorious HIV robs victims of their immune systems, leading to AIDS and eventual death.

Victims: Anyone engaged in any kind of sexual activity is fair game to Notorious HIV. This criminal isn't just America's Most Unwanted. He has an international network most prominent on the continent of Africa. It's estimated that there are 42 million people in the world living with HIV and that 3.2 million of them are under the age of 15. Since the beginning of the global epidemic, it's estimated that 24.8 million people have died from complications directly related to AIDS. Notorious HIV is known to prefer people who already have another STD—whether or not that STD causes open sores or breaks in the skin.

Crime Scene: Any broken skin or mucous membranes, including the mouth, eyes, nose, vagina, rectum and opening of the penis.

Modus Operandi: Vaginal sex, anal sex and oral sex. Body fluids, including blood, semen, vaginal fluid and breast milk, have been found to contain high concentrations of HIV. Notorious HIV operates through skin-to-skin contact with open sores and lesions. He can enter a victim through a vein (when sharing needles during drug injection). In addition, female victims can pass the disease to their babies before birth or through breast-feeding after birth.

Notorious HIV cannot be transmitted casually, so kissing on the cheek, hugs and handshakes are very safe. Open-mouth kissing is considered a low risk activity for Notorious HIV, but prolonged open-mouth kissing can allow Notorious HIV to spread and expand his crime network.

Evidence: Those who come into direct contact with Notorious HIV may initially experience flu-like symptoms, including fatigue, fever, aches and

Profile continued on next page.

rashes, for a short period of time. After the initial crime, most victims have no recognizable evidence for years. When the evidence goes undetected or unreported, the victim can become one of Notorious HIV's many unsuspecting accomplices by spreading the disease if he or she continues to engage in sexual activity.

The Crime: After initial flu-like symptoms, most victims have no signs of the crime (infection) for the first 10 years. By then, the victim's immune system is weakened enough to cause a variety of illnesses, including cancers, that eventually result in death.

Investigation: Blood test, oral fluid test or urine test between three and six months after the crime.

Apprehension: Since Notorious HIV is part of the Viral Family, he cannot be fully apprehended and cured. However, victims should seek an immediate medical examination if they have had sex with a partner who has been sexually active. There is no cure for HIV/AIDS, but early detection of a crime allows for more options for treatment and preventive measures that can increase the length and quality of life for the victim.

Prevention: The only way to totally avoid becoming infected with Notorious HIV is not to have sexual intercourse (vaginal, oral or anal), or by having sex within the context of a lifelong mutually faithful monogamous relationship (better known as marriage) with a partner who is not infected. Condoms may reduce the risk of becoming a victim, but they never eliminate it. See Self-Defense Manual.

Sources

Center for Disease Control and Prevention. "HIV and Its Transmission." http://www.cdc.gov/hiv/resources/factsheets/transmission.htm.

Davis, K. R., and S. C.Weller. "The Effectiveness of Condoms in Reducing Heterosexual Transmission of HIV," *Family Planning Perspectives,* 1999:31(6), pp. 272-279.

America's Most Unwanted

Profile: G-Dub, a.k.a. Human Papillomavirus

The Accused: G-Dub, a.k.a. Genital Warts or Human Papilloma-virus (HPV). Another potentially deadly member of the Viral Family, G-Dub has more than 100 different relatives known as *strains* who are partners in crime. At least 30 of these strains are sexually transmitted, and some are known to cause cancer in the genital area. G-Dub is known to sometimes leave a calling card at the scene of the crime: genital WMDs (warts of mass destruction).

Victims: Anyone engaged in any kind of sexual activity has a high risk of encountering G-Dub. At least 50 percent of sexually active men and women will have G-Dub at some point in their lives, and by the age of 50, at least 75 percent of women will be a victim of G-Dub. With 20 million crimes already under his belt in the United States, G-Dub gets around. Though not as famous as Notorious HIV, G-Dub infects 20 times as many victims and claims more than twice as many lives every year in the U.S.

Crime Scene: Genitals and genital area, anus and in/around the mouth.

Modus Operandi: G-Dub attacks through direct skin-to-skin contact during vaginal, anal or oral sex with an infected partner. When warts are present, G-Dub is more likely to spread, but even without any visible symptoms, he's likely to commit the crime.

Evidence: Most victims of G-Dub do not know they've been vandalized, but they can still become an accomplice to further crime and spread it to others. G-Dub lives in the skin or mucus membranes without any signs or symptoms, quietly waiting to infect another victim. Within a few weeks, months or even years, some victims notice soft, moist, pink or flesh-colored swellings in their genital or groin area. These bumps can be flat or raised, single or multiple, small or large and even broccoli and cauliflower shaped.

The Crime: The offense and consequences of G-Dub's undercover operation is that he can remain in the body of his victims and spread to countless other victims through sexual contact. Ten strains of G-Dub

Profile continued on next page.

have been known to lead to the development of cervical cancer.

Investigation: Visual inspection of criminal activity by G-Dub from a crime scene investigator (a trained medical professional). Some of G-Dub's activities can be very difficult to detect. A Pap test is recommended for female victims as a screening tool for cervical cancer and pre-cancerous changes in the cervix related to HPV.

Apprehension: Since G-Dub is part of the Viral Family, he cannot be completely apprehended or cured. Some people have one episode of genital warts while others have many recurrences. In most female victims, the infection eventually goes away on its own. However, victims should seek immediate medical treatment if any evidence has been found. Several treatment options are available for removing visible genital warts, including:

- Cryotherapy: liquid nitrogen is used to freeze off the warts
- TCA (trichloracetic acid): a chemical is used to remove the warts
- Electrocauthery: an electric current is used to burn off the warts
- Laser therapy: an intense light is used to destroy warts
- Surgical removal: a knife is used to remove warts
- Cream or gel: a topical cream/gel is used to remove external genital warts (*Note: Over-the-counter wart treatments should* not *be used in the genital area.*)

Prevention: G-Dub can strike both men's and women's genital areas whether or not they are covered by a condom. The only way to stop G-Dub's crime wave is to abstain from sexual intercourse or to choose to be in a long-term mutually monogamous relationship (better known as marriage) with a partner who has been tested and is known to be uninfected. See Self-Defense Manual.

Sources

American Social Health Association. "Genital Warts Q&A." http://www.ashastd.org/learn/learn_hpv_warts.cfm.

Centers for Disease Control and Prevention. "Genital HPV Infection Fact Sheet." http://www.cdc.gov/std/HPV/STDFact-HPV.htm.

Cervical Cancer Campaign. "HPV Frequently Asked Questions." http://www.cervicalcancercampaign.org/faqs.aspx.

America's Most Unwanted

Profile: Herp, a.k.a. Herpes

The Accused: Herp, a.k.a. Herpes. A popular member of the Viral Family, Herp's victims fall prey to one of two categories of crimes: Oral Herpes (Herpes Simplex Virus Type 1) and Genital Herpes (Herpes Simplex Virus Type 2). Both of Herp's virus types can occur in either the genital or oral area.

Victims: Anyone engaged in any kind of sexual activity can become a victim. Once Herp strikes, a person may become infected for life. At least 45 million people in the United States are victims of Herp. In fact, one in five people over the age of 11 has herpes. Approximately 70 percent of those infected by Herp will have recurrences. Some will have outbreaks throughout their lives, ranging from every few weeks to every few years.

Crime Scene: Genitals, face, lips, mouth. Oral sex with an infected victim can lead to lesions on the face, lips and inside the mouth.

Modus Operandi: Genital contact, oral sex and anal sex. Herp operates through skin-to-skin contact. Once he gains a foothold in a victim, he makes copies of himself and spreads throughout the body, where he will hide out until he's ready to launch another assault. When he's ready to attack, victims may or may not experience a noticeable outbreak.

Evidence: Herp's victims experience blisters in the genital area and/or around the face and mouth. Once the blisters break, they leave tender ulcers or sores that take several weeks to heal. While the initial infection usually heals in a few weeks, outbreaks of criminal activity (new sores) can occur at the original scene every few weeks or months. For some women, the burning is so intense during an outbreak that they can't urinate. Before an outbreak, victims may experience *prodrome*, a sensation that includes fever, chills, tingling, burning or pain.

The Crime: The offense and consequences of Herp include recurring blisters and burning sores that can be transmitted to sexual partners, as well as from a mother to her baby during childbirth. When Herp is

Profile continued on next page.

present during a delivery, doctors will almost always require a C-section to minimize the risk of infecting the child, which can lead to blindness or death.

Investigation: Blood tests, viral culture.

Apprehension: Since Herp is part of the Viral Family, he cannot be fully apprehended or cured. However, victims should seek immediate medical treatment when evidence has been found. Anti-viral medication can reduce the severity of the crime (infection) and shorten the duration of the outbreaks. Keeping the area as clean and dry as possible and allowing the crime area to get air can help speed the healing process. (*Note: Over-the-counter creams and/or ointments are* not *recommended for genital herpes, since they can interfere with the healing process and extend the outbreak.*)

Prevention: Condoms may reduce the risk of becoming a victim, but they never eliminate it. The only way to completely avoid Herp's invasion is to avoid sexual intercourse (vaginal, oral or anal), or by having sex within the context of a lifelong mutually faithful monogamous relationship (better known as marriage) with an uninfected partner. See Self-Defense Manual.

Sources

American Social Health Association. "Herpes Fast Facts." http://www.ashastd.org/herpes/herpes_learn.cfm.

Centers for Disease Control and Prevention. "Sexually Transmitted Diseases: Genital Herpes." http://www.cdc.gov/std/Herpes/default.htm.

—. "Genital Herpes Fact Sheet." http://www.cdc.gov/std/Herpes/STDFact-Herpes.htm.

Fleming, D. "Herpes Simplex Virus Type 2 in the United States, 1976-1994." *New England Journal of Medicine*, October 1997: 337(16), pp. 1105-1111.

National Coalition of STD Directors. "Quick Facts: Herpes Simplex Virus (HSV-2)." http://www.ncsddc.org/herpes_simplex.htm.

America's Most Unwanted

Profile: Medea, a.k.a. Chlamydia

The Accused: Medea, a.k.a. Chlamydia. The most popular member of the Bacterial Family, Medea is the most frequently reported bacterial STD in the United States. She's known as a "silent" disease because about 75 percent of female victims and 50 percent of male victims don't show any signs of criminal activity.

Victims: Anyone engaged in any kind of sexual activity is fair game for Medea. With more than 2.8 million new victims each year, she is a hardened criminal and likes to prey on youth. Her prime victims are women ages 15 to 19 years of age. It's estimated that 10 percent of all sexually active teenagers are Medea's victims and at risk of infertility.

Crime Scene: Genitals and genital area, mouth and anus.

Modus Operandi: Genital contact, oral sex and anal sex.

Evidence: Men often have a hard time recognizing that Medea has perpetrated a crime. A few may experience some discharge from their penis or pain during urination, but most won't see a single shred of evidence that Medea has struck. They can quickly become accomplices spreading the disease to others if they continue sexual activity. Three-quarters of women who are victims don't show any evidence and don't know they are infected. Any recognizable criminal activity will appear during the first three weeks of infection. Signs of such activity include a vaginal discharge or a burning sensation while urinating. If the infection spreads to the fallopian tubes, a woman may experience lower abdominal pain, lower pack pain, bleeding between periods, pain during intercourse, nausea or fatigue.

The Crime: Medea strikes men, women and children. If undetected in men, Medea can cause inflammation of the prostate gland, scarring of the urethra, and infertility. If undetected in women, pelvic inflammatory disease can set in, resulting in infertility. Medea can also strike during childbirth, infecting babies through infected mothers and resulting in early infant pneumonia and conjunctivitis (pink eye) in newborns. In addition,

Profile continued on next page.

female victims are up to five times more likely to become infected with the Notorious HIV if exposed to Chlamydia, and they are also more likely to be a victim of Rhea, a.k.a. Gonorrhea.

Investigation: Tests options include urine and swab tests, among others.

Apprehension: Since she is part of the Bacterial Family, Medea can be apprehended and cured once detected. However, damage already incurred—such as infertility—cannot be reversed. Victims should seek immediate medical treatment if Medea is a suspect. Her criminal activity can be easily treated and cured with antibiotics.

Prevention: Condoms, if used correctly 100 percent of the time, may reduce the risk of infection by less than 50 percent. Those are bad odds when it comes to being a victim of Medea. The only way to totally avoid infection is to avoid sexual intercourse (vaginal, oral or anal) or by having sex within the context of a lifelong mutually faithful monogamous relationship (better known as marriage) with an uninfected partner. If a person has had sex before marriage, he or she should be tested, regardless of whether that person is a man or a woman (see Self-Defense Manual).

Sources

Ahmed, S., T. Lutalo, M. Waver, et al. "HIV Incidence and Sexually Transmitted Disease Prevalence Associated with Condom Use: A Population Study in Rakai, Uganda." *AIDS*. 2001:15, pp. 2171-2179.

Centers for Disease Control and Prevention. "Sexually Transmitted Diseases: Chlamydia." http://www.cdc.gov/std/chlamydia/default.htm.

America's Most Unwanted

Profile: Rhea, a.k.a. Gonorrhea

The Accused: Rhea, a.k.a. Gonorrhea. A popular member of the Viral Family, she likes to commit her crimes in warm, most areas and tends to multiply wherever she goes.

Victims: Anyone engaged in any kind of sexual activity can run into Rhea. She strikes more than 700,000 unsuspecting victims in the United States each year, but only half of the victims report the crime (infection). Rhea's highest reported crime rates are among sexually active teenagers, young adults and African Americans. Newborns also become innocent victims as women pass the bacteria to their babies during delivery, resulting in infant blindness, joint infection, and/or a life-threatening blood infection.

Crime Scene: Crimes are committed in the genitals and genital area, including the uterus (womb) and fallopian tubes (egg canals) in female victims and the urethra (urine canal) in male and female victims. Rhea can also commit crimes in the mouth, throat and eyes.

Modus Operandi: Rhea strikes through contact with the penis, vagina, anus or mouth. She can also spread her crime from mother to baby during delivery.

Evidence: Though many male victims don't show any evidence or symptoms that they've been attacked, some experience a burning sensation when urinating or a white, yellow or green discharge from the penis during the first month after the crime has been committed. In addition, some male victims get painful or swollen testicles.

Though many female victims don't show any signs or symptoms of criminal activity, they can experience a burning sensation during urination, increased vaginal discharge or bleeding between periods. These signs can often be mistaken for a bladder or vaginal infection.

Symptoms of rectal infection in male and female victims may include discharge, anal itching, soreness, bleeding or painful bowel movements. Criminal activity in the mouth may cause sore throat.

Profile continued on next page.

The Crime: In female victims, Rhea leaves a trail in the form of pelvic inflammatory disease (PID). Signs of this crime include abdominal pain, fever, internal abscesses (pus-filled pockets that are difficult to cure) and chronic pelvic pain. This brutal disease can lead to infertility as well as a life-threatening pregnancy abnormality that causes a fertilized egg to grow outside the uterus. Rhea can also spread her crimes to the blood and joints, occasionally leading to death. Rhea's partner in crime is Medea (a.k.a. Chlamydia) and they often travel together. In addition, victims of Rhea are more likely to be victims of her deadly associate, Notorious HIV, and spread his crimes to others.

Investigation: Several laboratory tests are available, including a urine test.

Apprehension: Since she is part of the Bacterial Family, Rhea can usually be fully apprehended (cured). Antibiotics can successfully arrest her, but several drug-resistant strains are more difficult to cure. While medication can stop the criminal activity, it will not repair permanent damage done by the crime. Any genital symptom such as discharge, burning during urination, sores or rashes is a sign to stop having sex and see a health care professional immediately. Victims should notify all recent sex partners as soon as possible.

Prevention: Latex condoms may reduce the risk of transmission of Rhea, but the only way to stop Rhea's crime wave completely is to abstain from sexual intercourse or to have sex in a long-term mutually monogamous relationship (better known as marriage) with a partner who has been tested and is known to be uninfected. See Self-Defense Manual.

Source

Centers for Disease Control and Prevention. "Sexually Transmitted Diseases: Gonorrhea." http://www.cdc.gov/std/Gonorrhea/.

America's Most Unwanted

Profile: Trixie, a.k.a. Trichomoniasis

The Accused: Trixie, a.k.a. Trichomoniasis. A key leader of gangs and cell groups, she is a complete parasite of a criminal.

Victims: Anyone engaged in any kind of sexual activity is inviting Trixie to commit a crime. Trixie is a popular criminal among women and finds more than 7.8 million new victims each year. She is the most easily apprehended criminal among young sexually active women.

Crime Scene: Genitals and genital area, mouth and anus.

Modus Operandi: Genital contact, oral sex.

Evidence: Trixie rarely leaves signs of her criminal activity on male victims. Occasionally, a male may have temporary irritation inside the penis, mild discharge or slight burning after urination or ejaculation. Within 5 to 28 days of the crime, female victims often have a frothy, yellow-green vaginal discharge with a strong odor. They may experience discomfort during intercourse and urination, as well as irritation and itching of the genital area. Occasional lower abdominal pain can occur.

The Crime: Trixie is known for the discomfort she causes her victims, including discharge, burning during urination, sores, rashes and pain. Pregnant victims may have babies who are born early or with low birth weights. Trixie can increase a female victim's chances of attack by Notorious HIV and—if she continues her sexual activity—spreading him to others.

Investigation: Physical examination and laboratory test.

Apprehension: Since Trixie is a leader of bacterial gangs and cell groups, she can be fully apprehended (cured). However, victims should seek immediate medical treatment when evidence has been found. Victims may be treated with a prescription drug.

Prevention: Latex condoms may reduce the risk of transmission of Trixie, but the only way to stop her crime wave completely is to abstain

Profile continued on next page.

from sexual intercourse or have sex in a long-term mutually monogamous relationship (better known as marriage) with a partner who has been tested and is known to be uninfected. See Self-Defense Manual.

Sources

Centers for Disease Control and Prevention. "Sexually Transmitted Diseases: Trichomoniasis." http://www.cdc.gov/std/trichomonas/default.htm.

Sorvillo, F., L. Smith, , P. Krendt, et al. "Trichomonas Vaginalis, HIV, and African-Americans." *Emerging Infectious Diseases*, 2001:7(6), pp. 927-932.

America's Most Unwanted

Profile: P-Deasy, a.k.a. PID (Pelvic Inflammatory Disease)

The Accused: P-Deasy, a.k.a. PID (Pelvic Inflammatory Disease). P-Deasy is known as a hardened criminal and is the leading cause of infertility (the inability to have children) among women.

Victims: Women engaged in any kind of sexual activity are fair game for P-Deasy. This villain has a number of partners in crime, including Medea (Chlamydia) and Rhea (Gonorrhea). They often travel together, though other bacteria can also invite P-Deasy to a crime scene. P-Deasy's prime victims are women between the ages of 15 and 25 years old. He is known to attack this age group more than any other. More than 100,000 women lose the ability to have children every year as a result of P-Deasy's criminal behavior.

Crime Scene: Genital area and reproductive organs.

Modus Operandi: Genital contact, oral sex and anal sex.

Evidence: P-Deasy is hard to recognize, but some of his criminal trademark signs include dull pain or tenderness in the lower abdomen, burning or pain during urination, nausea, vomiting, bleeding between menstrual periods, increased or changed vaginal discharge, pain during sex, fever or chills. Occasionally P-Deasy won't leave any evidence or will confuse medical investigators by masquerading as appendicitis, ectopic (tubal) pregnancy, ruptured ovarian cysts, or other problems.

The Crime: The consequences of undetected P-Deasy can remain in the bodies of his victims and lead to infertility, inflammation of the urinary tract and bladder, ectopic (tubal) pregnancy, and chronic pelvic pain. In addition, an abscess (pus-filled area) can develop within the pelvic region.

Investigation: Pelvic exam and/or pelvic ultrasound, laparoscopy.

Apprehension: Though P-Deasy is part of the bacterial gangs and cell groups, he can be cured with several types of antibiotics. However, antibiotic treatment does not reverse any damage that has already

---

Profile continued on next page.

occurred to the reproductive organs. The longer a victim delays treatment, the more likely she is to become infertile or have a future ectopic (tubal) pregnancy due to damage on the fallopian tubes.

Prevention: Untreated STDs, including Medea (Chlamydia) and Rhea (Gonorrhea), are the main villains behind P-Deasy's infiltration, and they should be apprehended immediately. Latex condoms may reduce the eventual development of P-Deasy, but the only way to stop P-Deasy's crime wave completely is to abstain from sexual intercourse or to have sex in a long-term mutually monogamous relationship (better known as marriage) with a partner who has been tested and is known to be uninfected. Sex partners of PID victims should be examined and treated if they have had recent sexual contact to avoid reinfection. See Self-Defense Manual.

Sources

American Social Health Association. "PID Q&A." http://www.ashastd.org/learn/learn_pid.cfm.

Centers for Disease Control and Prevention. "Pelvic Inflammatory Disease Fact Sheet." http://www.cdc.gov/std/PID/STDFact-PID.htm.

America's Most Unwanted

Profile: The Crabs, a.k.a. Pubic Lice

The Accused: The Crabs, a.k.a. Pubic Lice. Though this gang comes from the same crime family of parasites as head and body lice, they are not the same thing. The Crabs resemble crabs you see on the beach, and they're often whitish-gray or rust colored. They often leave their small, oval-shaped, pearl-colored eggs at the base of the hair.

Victims: In the United States, The Crabs commit crimes against three million victims each year.

Crime Scene: Pubic hair and other course hair, including eyelashes, eyebrows, facial hair, chest or armpits. The Crabs do not usually commit their crimes in hair on the head.

Modus Operandi: Genital contact, oral sex and anal sex. Non-sexual crimes are also possible. The Crabs can attack victims who sleep in an infested bed, use an infested towel, wear infested clothing, or use an infested toilet seat (though this is rare). The Crabs are thieves. They steal human blood in order to survive and can live up to 24 hours after feasting on the human body.

Evidence: The Crabs criminal presence is often recognized by itching in the pubic area. The itching is caused by an allergic reaction to the activity of The Crabs and usually begins within five days of the crime. In addition, dark or bluish spots may appear in the infested area—a result of the bites. A magnifying glass can help identify the perpetrator as The Crabs.

The Crime: The offense and consequences of an undetected presence of The Crabs is discomfort, inconvenience and potential embarrassment. Occasionally, secondary bacterial infections may occur due to aggressive scratching.

Investigation: Visual inspection with a magnifying glass or examination by a crime scene investigator (a health care professional).

Apprehension: Since The Crabs are linked to the bacterial gangs and cell groups, they can be fully apprehended (cured). However, victims should

Profile continued on next page.

seek immediate medical treatment when evidence has been found. A prescription shampoo is available as well as an over-the-counter cream, Permethrin. Neither should be used on the eyebrows or eyelashes.

Prevention: The only way to stop The Crabs' crime wave is to abstain from sexual intercourse or to have sex in a long-term mutually monogamous relationship (better known as marriage) with a partner who has been tested and is known to be uninfected. See Self-Defense Manual.

Sources

American Social Health Association. "Crabs Fast Facts." http://www.ashastd.org/learn/learn_crabs_facts.cfm.

Centers for Disease Control and Prevention. "Pubic Lice Infestation Fact Sheet." http://www.cdc.gov/ncidod/dpd/parasites/lice/factsht_pubic_lice.htm.

America's Most Unwanted

Profile: HB, a.k.a. Hepatitis B

The Accused: HB, a.k.a. Hepatitis B. HB is a member of the Viral Family and is commonly spread through sexual contact. One of his brothers, Hepatitis C, can also commit crimes through sexual contact.

Victims: Anyone engaged in any kind of sexual activity is fair game to HB. One out of 20 people in the U.S. will be a victim of HB during his or her lifetime. The CDC estimates that 1.25 million people in the United States are victims of a chronic HB crime.

Crime Scenes: The liver, which becomes inflamed.

Modus Operandi: Vaginal, anal or oral sex. HB invades through contact with another person's blood, including blood transfusions, contaminated needles, razors and knives. Pregnant victims of HB can pass it on to their babies at birth.

Evidence: The CDC estimates that 30 percent of HB's victims have no signs or symptoms that a crime has been committed. Victims who do experience signs usually experience flu-like symptoms including fatigue, mild fever, nausea, vomiting and discomfort in the abdomen between 9 and 21 weeks after exposure. Loss of appetite and weight loss may result. Victims may notice dark colored urine and their skin may become yellow.

The Crime: It's estimated that 15 to 25 percent of HB's victims die each year in the United States due to complications of cirrhosis and liver cancer. HB can cause lifelong infection, cirrhosis (scarring of the liver, liver cancer, liver failure), as well as death. HB victims may become accomplices if they continue sexual activity, spreading the disease. Pregnant women may also infect their babies.

Investigation: Blood test.

Apprehension: Since HB is part of the Viral Family, he cannot be fully apprehended and cured. Victims should seek an immediate medical examination if they have had sex with another partner who has been

Profile continued on next page.

sexually active. There is no cure for HB, but early detection of a crime allows for more treatment options, including antiviral drugs to treat chronic HB infection.

Prevention: Latex condoms may reduce the crime of HB and there is a Hepatitis B vaccine, but the only way to stop HB's crime wave completely is to abstain from sexual intercourse or to have sex in a long-term mutually monogamous relationship (better known as marriage) with a partner who has been tested and is known to be uninfected. Sex partners of victims who have contracted HB should be examined and treated if they have had recent sexual contact to avoid reinfection. See Self-Defense Manual.

Sources

American Social Health Association. "Hepatitis B Q&A." http://www.ashastd.org/learn/learn_hepatitisB.cfm.

Centers for Disease Control and Prevention. "Viral Hepatitis B." http://www.cdc.gov/ncidod/diseases/hepatitis/b/index.htm.

National Organization of STD Directors. "Hepatitis B Quick Facts." http://www.ncsddc.org/hepatitis_b.htm.

CHAPTER 5

I'll Just Practice Safe Sex

My friend Luis says there's no such thing as safe sex—and he is living proof. Check this out:

> I was born in El Salvador and the thing I remember most is that I didn't have a father. My parents got divorced when I was two. All my life I looked up to my older brother as my mentor in life. I was always trying to imitate my brother. He got involved in drugs, sex, alcohol and violence at a very young age. At the age of 12, I started having sex. My first time was with a prostitute. My brother's older friends promised to make me a man through the experience, but instead, I just became a sex addict.
>
> When the prostitute asked if I was ready, I said yes and when we were finished she said, "Next." So I started treating every girl I slept with that way. That went on until I was 16, when I got my girlfriend pregnant. By the time I found out, she had already had an abortion. We

started dating again, and she became pregnant again. This time we got married and moved to the States. I didn't have an education, so I started working cleaning tables. By the time I was 18, we divorced. I started paying $400 a month in child support.

At 22, I did it again. We were married and within two years, we decided to divorce. There was no love; it was all about the sex. Right when we were deciding to get separated, we found out she was pregnant again. My friend encouraged me to ask my wife to get an abortion because if I didn't I would have to pay more money. She agreed.

I wish I could say I learned my lesson, but at 29 I did it again. So I had three kids with three different women, killed two babies and was paying child support. It turns out that I wasn't too different from my brother: He had three kids with three different women.

> *Luis says he has five reasons why condoms aren't safe: his three living kids and two aborted babies, all conceived while he was using condoms.*

One of my deep convictions about American culture is that we are deeply immersed in what I call "the Matrix." This might sound familiar to you unless you were one of the two people who didn't see the science fiction cult classic film *The Matrix*, starring Keanu Reeves. The film depicts a futuristic world where human bodies have been suspended in a comatose state while their minds are imprisoned in a world of unreality.

A small resistance group dedicates itself to freeing the human race from captivity. The first episode in the trilogy is my favorite, not just because its themes are analogous to the story of Christ, but also because I believe it's a pretty fair depiction of our culture on many levels, including our beliefs about sex. Every lie in truth's clothing that we believe attests to how deeply we are entrenched in the Matrix, and every Naked Truth that is revealed frees us from the lies that keep us trapped in unreality—an unreality that ultimately leads to death and destruction.

> If the truth can set you free, how much more will a lie keep you in bondage?

Abraham Lincoln is often quoted as saying, "The truth shall set you free," but it was Jesus Christ who said it first. Most people actually misquote this line, because He actually said, "The truth shall *make* you free" (John 8:32, *NKJV*, emphasis added). You can be *set* free and choose to stay in the cage, but truth *makes* you free—my job is to turn your cage upside down and shake it until you fall out!

I like to ask my audiences who it was that said, "If you tell a big enough lie, tell it over and over again, over a long enough period of time, the masses of people will begin to believe that it is the truth."

Needless to say, I get a wide variety of responses including Albert Einstein, Dr. Martin Luther King, Jr., past and present presidents, as well as an occasional Michael Jackson. But there is usually one extremely bright student who provides an answer that shocks and dismays his fellow classmates: Adolph Hitler.

Though Hitler is credited with this quote, it was actually said by his chief propagandist, Joseph Goebbels—but "Hitler" is close enough for me to applaud any student who comes up with this answer!

We have been brainwashed, just like Adolph Hitler brainwashed his own people. Have you ever seen the TV show *The Dog Whisperer*? This guy, Cesar Millan, is a dog-training expert, and I swear . . . it seems like he actually knows how to speak Dog (Dog-lish? Dog-ese?). The Dog Whisperer specializes in retraining "bad" older dogs. Do you know why those older dogs are "bad"? Because they weren't trained properly when they were young!

The best time to train a dog is when he's young, before he learns bad habits. How do you train him? You tell him what you want to do and then you give him a demonstration of what you want him to do. Over a period of time, given the correct stimulus, he'll respond exactly the way you've programmed him to respond. When you tell the animal to sit, he will sit. When you tell the dog to bark, he will bark. And when you tell him to roll over, he'll roll over. The Dog Whisperer knows that what you train is what you get.

The Naked Truth is that there is no such thing as safe sex. That's a lie in truth's clothing.

The way you're trained is the way you'll behave. In America, if you're young, you're expected to act like an animal, so you have been trained to practice something called *safe*_____ (fill in the blank). That's right. They encourage us to practice *safe sex*—but The Naked Truth is that there is no such thing as safe sex. That is a lie in truth's clothing. It's true that condoms are saf*er* than no protection at all, but the safest sex is abstinence, or what some people call "saved sex."

> *Policymakers should be talking about 'safer sex,' not safe sex, when speaking of condoms.*—Norman Hearst, professor at the University of California at San Francisco[1]

A while back, I had a wonderful conversation with a gentleman who is one of the world's leading authorities on condoms. His name is Dr. Thomas Fitch, also known as The Condom King. Dr. Fitch challenged the U.S. Food and Drug Administration (FDA) and the Centers for Disease Control (CDC) and demanded that they release information about condoms to the general public. The information revealed showed that there was no evidence that *condoms reduced the risk of HPV infection.*[2] In other words, condoms were ruled ineffective in preventing the transmission of the most common viral STD.

If you don't get nothin' else, I need you to get this: If you decide you are going to start or to continue having sex outside of marriage, there is a 50/50 chance that you will get at least one STD in your lifetime. Odds are that it's going to be one of the most common STDs, and if it's a virus, chances are it will be human papillomavirus, or genital warts. It's the most common viral STD and it is nasty, to say the least. If you get genital warts, you're going to start growing warts in your genital area. Yeah, and I don't mean one or two little warts. They grow on top of each other, and they'll begin to form nodules and clusters that look like broccoli. They're called condyloma. They make it painful to sit and painful to walk. And they're most painful when they're being removed.

A good friend of mine served as a doctor on a naval ship in Southern California. On Fridays, the doctor dedicated the entire day to wart removal for the 20 or so gentlemen who lined up outside his door. Mind you, these were not the same 20 gentlemen every week—it was a revolving door: a different group coming to get their warts removed each week! If you were one of those unlucky men, you'd go into the doc's office, take off all your clothes and put on that little paper gown with your butt hanging out the back.

Then you'd have to choose which way you want your genital warts removed. First, you could have them burned off with a laser. Or if you prefer, you could have the doctor take an eyedropper and burn each wart off one by one with acid. (If you think that area is sensitive now, just wait till you got acid and laser burns on it. Uh-huh. Remember when you were little and you fell down and you got a booboo? And Momma used to kiss it? Well, she ain't kissing this one!)

But even after all that pain and misery, you wouldn't be done. As those burned spots began to heal, scabs would form on top of each one. When the skin heals up, the scab falls off and you'd have perfectly normal-looking skin. But guess what happens over time? The warts grow back. They never die. They just multiply.

The Naked Truth is that you can't tell if you're going to get genital warts just by looking, and condoms can't always protect you from getting them.

You may think everything looks all right down there. And maybe, if you're a guy, you think you'll just strap on some extra protection—you'll wear a coupla condoms instead of just one (which isn't recommended, by the way). But sex is messy, and a condom can't protect from all the fluids being exchanged. Even if you put on a hundred condoms and none of them happens to tear, leak, break or slip off, and the person that you're with has the virus . . . guess what? You can still get genital warts. Everything can look alright down there when a person is between their acid and laser treatments and the skin is healed up, but they can be growing warts on the inside where you can't see them! Now does that sound like safe sex? I don't think so. That's why you've got to start making some decisions now about abstinence.

Genital warts aren't the only reason sex outside of marriage isn't safe. HIV/AIDS is a pandemic (a disease that is literally devastating whole populations around the world). In the U.S., AIDS gets most of the press, but other STDs are far more contagious. A cut or an abrasion has to be accessible for HIV to get in, but with HPV and a few of the others, skin-to-skin contact is enough to pass on the infection. People think, "Well, it's all about safe sex, so I'll put a condom on and everything will be okay." That is a lie in truth's clothing. You may be *safer*, but there are some fatal and deadly STDs that a condom just can't protect you from.

I was walking to the store the other day and I heard the two girls who work behind the counter talking about what kind of birth control to get—whether an IUD, a Depo-Provera injection or the patch. They were just going on and on and finally I said, "Okay, and what happens when you get AIDS? How is the patch gonna help you?"

The chances of getting an STD are greater than the chances of pregnancy. You can do the patch, the pill, the shot or some other form of birth control, but guess what? None of them are a 100 percent effective in preventing pregnancy, and none of them are 100 percent effective in preventing STDs. The only way to guarantee that you will not get pregnant or an STD is abstinence.

> One-third of teens in America and two-thirds of all young adults have admitted to having oral sex.

You may be thinking that there are ways around STDs and pregnancy with alternatives like oral sex. Some people try to say that oral sex isn't sex, but what's the noun in "oral sex"? *Sex!* Lots of people think that oral sex is not a big deal. As a matter of fact, one-third of teens in America and two-thirds of all young adults have admitted to having oral sex. But if it's not a big deal, why is it that every single sexually transmitted disease can be caught by engaging in oral sex?

There is no such thing as safe sex—that's just a lie in latex clothing. There is such a thing as saf*er* sex, but the only safe sex is to abstain from sex until marriage and marry someone else who has done the same. This notion is not obvious to everyone. It certainly wasn't obvious the first time I went to testify in Washington, D.C., before a Senate subcommittee chaired by Senator Orin Hatch.

I was the director of Athletes for Abstinence, which was a part of A.C. Green's youth foundation in Los Angeles. (Green played basketball for the L.A. Lakers at the time.) We were preparing to embark on the "It Ain't Worth It" campaign with a few pro-athlete friends of ours, including NBA All-Star David Robinson (San Antonio Spurs) and All-Pro Darryl Greene (Washington Redskins), the fastest man in the NFL. We received an invitation to testify before the Senate Appropriations Committee on the topic of teen pregnancy. I was sent as the representative and I had no idea what I was in for.

I was the last person to speak in a long line of MDs, PhDs and the former Surgeon General herself, Joycelyn Elders. I was definitely the new kid on the block and everyone's junior by at least 20 years—I could recognize a token gesture when I saw one. I thought I would be nervous, but on the contrary, I couldn't wait to sit before our nation's elected leaders to testify. I had no reason to be fearful or nervous. I had no tenure at a university to lose, I wasn't the recipient of any government grants that were in jeopardy, and furthermore, I had the truth.

I was not impressed by the testimonies of most of the witnesses. When they were questioned by a few senators, they gave some of the weakest and most contradictory answers I had ever heard. It became quite apparent that this entire day was just a formality . . . but then my turn came.

My first statement addressed the obvious: The issue is not teens getting pregnant, but teens having sex! Anytime you start with the wrong question, you inevitably get the wrong answer. Because the Senate committee asked the wrong question, "How do we reduce teen pregnancy?" they ended up with the wrong answer: "Let's teach them how not to get pregnant."

The former Surgeon General suggested that Norplant (birth control implants) and Depo-Provera should be introduced to inner-city girls, to which I responded, "AIDS doesn't care about Norplant." I wasn't surprised by Dr. Elders's suggestion, because she was the same person who proposed we teach young people what to do in the backseat of a car, since we teach them what to do in the front seat in driver's education. *Hello!* Has she forgotten—or maybe it was not required in her day—that you must be a *licensed* driver to get behind the wheel of a car? Although she appeared to be an advocate of abstinence, Dr. Elders was actually a strong proponent of "outercourse."

This may be confusing to some of you. It certainly was to the senators that day, so I took it upon myself to clarify it for them. From Dr. Elders's office, I acquired a list of about 20 things that she qualified as "outercourse" (an alternative to intercourse). I read all 20 activities aloud to the senators and many turned red from embarrassment. The activities included taking showers together, mutual masturbation and dry humping.[3]

If you think these few items are offensive—good. These were the *least* offensive outercourse activities on the list, and Dr. Elders suggested that they should be taught to kids in grades K through 12!

It's likely that her statements that day were just a few in a long line of comments that ultimately led to her removal from the office of Surgeon General a few weeks later. Many of you may have never heard of Joycelyn Elders, and she is a long-forgotten thought to a few, but trust me—she hasn't faded away. Just recently she wrote the foreword to a book that suggests that intergenerational sex is acceptable. If you haven't figured out what this phrase "intergenerational" means, let's just say Dr. Elders and R. Kelly might get along really well. Or maybe not—I think she is way over his age preference.

Eventually that day in the Senate committee hearing, the elephant under the rug was addressed—the issue of condoms came up. I had to ask the obvious: Why aren't young people being told the truth about safe sex? I don't know about you, but when I look up "safe" in *Webster's Dictionary*, I read, "free from harm, injury, risk or danger." If you put the word "safe" next to the word "sex," the message is that you can engage in sex that is safe from harm, sex that is free from injury, sex that is free from risk, and sex that is free from danger.

Someday soon I'll turn this point into its own pamphlet. It will be called *Oh, Snap!*

Safe, Safer or Not Safe at All?

When asked about the best way to prevent pregnancy and STDs, most people will say condoms. But have you ever read a condom package? Manufacturers won't say that their product *prevents* anything. The best you get from one popular brand is "*If* used properly, latex condoms will *help* to *reduce* the risk of transmission of HIV infection (AIDS) and many other sexually transmitted diseases. Also highly effective against pregnancy. Caution: this product contains natural rubber latex which may cause allergic reactions" (emphasis added).

You don't have to be an English major to note that "help" means *assist* and "reduce" means *lower*. Put together, "assist in lowering" doesn't sound anything like "prevent," which means *stop*! It seems to me that the caution warning should go at the beginning of the label, considering the chance of contracting a deadly virus is far greater than having an allergic reaction to rubber latex.

When asked about the safety success rate for condoms, most people will give a 97 to 99.9 percent figure, but from what I understand, this rate is accurate for a laboratory setting. If any of the randomly selected 100 condoms springs a leak when filled with water, it is assumed that the other 98 or 99 are okay. I don't know of anybody who makes water balloons out of condoms. In the real world, condoms fail anywhere between 8 and 14 percent of the time. The result is usually pregnancy. The younger the user, the higher the failure rate.[4]

The label on the back of a condom says that it's effective against "many other STDs," but they forget to tell you that among the "many," there are deadly STDs other than HIV/AIDS against which condoms give virtually no protection. Even President Clinton recognized the importance of condom safety. He directed the FDA to ensure that condom labels were medically accurate regarding their overall effectiveness or *lack of effectiveness* in preventing infection with STDs, *including* HPV.[5]

Although certain cosmetics, food, and over-the-counter drugs must be approved by the U.S. Food and Drug Administration (FDA), condoms—which are the top-recommended barrier between life and death—have yet to see the words "FDA approved" on the packaging.

Does any of this sound safe to you? It may sound saf*er* than nothing at all—but playing Russian roulette with only one bullet instead of a fully-loaded revolver is safer, too. It's just a matter of time before—*Oh, snap!*—the condom breaks.

Human Papillo-*what?*

Until recently I would say, "Human papillomavirus, or HPV" and most people would say "HP-huh?" It is a mouthful, but it is far more prevalent in the United States than HIV/AIDS. HPV claims thousands of lives every year.[6] In fact, HPV has been detected in virtually all invasive cervical cancers and has been confirmed as the major cause of this cancer.[7]

The National Cervical Cancer Public Education Campaign asserts that HPV is one of the most common STDs in the United States. An estimated 24 million Americans are infected, with the frequency of infection and disease appearing to increase.[8] The CDC notes that "The most reliable means of preventing sexual transmission of genital HPV infection is likely to be abstinence, although non-sexual routes of transmission are possible."[9] In many studies, condoms have been found ineffective to prevent the transmission of HPV.[10]

You don't ever hear this on the new HPV commercial: "You can get cancer from a virus? Gee, I didn't know that." Of course you didn't know, because no one is talking about it. They never mention how you get the virus or how you can prevent acquiring the virus.

The U.S. House of Representatives drafted a bill several years ago with a provision mandating that all condoms include a warning label instructing that they are unable to effectively prevent the spread of the human papillomavirus (HPV), which leads to virtually all cases of cervical cancer. These labels would be much like those on cigarette packages warning smokers about lung cancer. Similarly, these warning labels on condom packages would increase the awareness of HPV and cervical cancer, and inform the purchaser that condom use does not protect against HPV infection. But wouldn't you know it? The bill was opposed by some policymakers who argued such language would create unfounded hysteria and would discourage the use of condoms, which are effective in reducing incidents of "many other STDs."

Well, what do you know . . . there's that phrase "many other STDs" again. Wouldn't you think that the most common viral STD—which is more contagious than HIV/AIDS—would get a little more respect and maybe some preferential treatment? Not a chance: The Senate passed the bill, but it didn't include the mandated warning label.[11]

Every true abstinence educator that I have met takes painstaking efforts to use the same research sources the condom people do: CDC (Center for Disease Control), NIH (National Institute for Health), DHHS (U.S. Department of Health and Human Services), etc. Yet condoms, which have been pushed as "safe sex" for years, are the most medically inaccurate and deceptive notion presented to the American public—particularly its youth, who think of the condom as the silver bullet, the panacea, or what they unwittingly refer to as "protection."

> *If you can't suppress the truth, destroy evidence of the truth.*
> —Unknown

It's as Simple as ABc

All of us in the States have heard about the AIDS pandemic on the continent of Africa, but most of us have never heard of the success story in Uganda: It has experienced the greatest decline in HIV prevalence of any country in the world.[12]

Beginning in the mid-1980s, the Ugandan government, working closely with community and faith-based organizations, delivered a consistent AIDS-prevention message to the

Ugandan people: ***A***bstain from sex until marriage, ***B***e faithful to your partner, or use ***c***ondoms (note the little *c*) if abstinence and fidelity are not practiced.

I was recently asked by the Ambassador of Uganda to speak at a reception honoring their president, Yoweri Museveni, for his work in AIDS. Hearing him explain the ABc model was vastly different than hearing the pro-condom faction encourage the abC model. To hear them tell it, A, B and C are three equally valid choices, with C being the most logical and effective.

President Musevini explained that ABC is actually ABc, with condoms given the least attention and emphasis. ***Abstinence until marriage*** is the main message, then ***Be** faithful in marriage*, and last, *use **condoms*** for two segments of society: a) married couples who know one is HIV-positive and do not want to risk infecting the uninfected spouse, and b) those who are unlikely to change their behavior, such as prostitutes. Musevini went on to explain that although prostitution was not an acceptable career choice, prostitutes were highly encouraged to use condoms in order that they may survive long enough to hear the gospel of Jesus Christ to change their lives.

Whether or not you agree with his view of condoms as a stopgap measure, all reports agree on one central fact: Abstinence and faithfulness—not condoms—were by far the most important factors in the decline of HIV in Uganda.[13] Edward C. Green, a senior research scientist at Harvard and author of *Rethinking AIDS Prevention*, said, "The Ugandan model has the most to teach the rest of the world."[14]

Not long after meeting President Musevini, I had a private dinner with his ambassador to the U.S. at the Ugandan Embassy. I was further astounded by the testimony of Ambassador Ssempala about her nation's turnaround, and how the youth are the ones who are now leading the way. It blows me away that I have not heard any of this in the mainstream press! All the coverage about the solution to AIDS in Africa has been about condoms.

The Washington Post recently quoted enthusiastic health care workers when they talked about condoms but omitted testimony from government officials about the emphasis on sexual abstinence and faithfulness.[15] It seems that it's popular to ignore the success of the safest sex program in the world, even though there have been numerous independent studies from medical journals and data from such organizations as the Harvard Center for Population and Developmental Studies, the World Health Organization (WHO), the Joint United Nations Program on HIV/AIDS (UNAIDS), and the Ugandan government itself—all documenting the ABc program's achievements. The effectiveness of this approach has all but been ignored in the U.S. The question is, *Why?*

> *We are being told that only a thin piece of rubber stands between us and the death of our continent.*—Yoweri Museveni, President of Uganda

The back of a condom package only offers words of uncertainty: "*If* used properly, latex condoms will *help* to *reduce* the risk of transmission of HIV infection (AIDS) and many other sexually transmitted diseases" (emphasis added). God's Word, in contrast, offers certainty: "*If* you abide in my word, you are my disciples *indeed* . . . And you shall know the truth and the truth *shall make* you free" (John 8:31-32, *NKJV*, emphasis added).

If you're having sex—protected or not—outside of marriage, then you aren't abiding in His Word, because He is the Word and His Word is the truth. Being a disciple means that you not only mentally assent to what His Word says, but that you live it as well. After all, "discipline" is derived from the word *disciple.*

The Bible says, "the truth shall make you free." But there may be a few of you who are still saying, "Well you've told me the truth about condoms, and I still don't think any differently." If that's you, think about this: The New Testament was originally written in Greek and has been translated so that we can read it in our own language. The Greek word for "know" in this passage means *to have intimate fellowship with*—fellowship so intimate, in fact, that it is the same word for *intercourse*, as in "Adam knew Eve." To "know" the Truth intimately (that is, the Word of God, Jesus) requires you to be intimate with Him in a way that demands exclusivity—that you don't *know* anybody else (besides your spouse after marriage). If you are in bondage to sex, you aren't free to know the Truth.

If you are an unmarried professing Christian and you are having sex, there is some bondage breaking that needs to happen, because Jesus not only came to forgive our sins but to also set the captives free. Many people know that "Thou shall not commit adultery" is the seventh commandment—but are you *living* it?

Ask Yourself

- Is there such a thing as *safe sex*? Why or why not?
- Why do you think people believe the lie that sex can be safe? What would you say to someone who believes in safe sex?
- List two facts about STDs that you didn't know before you read this chapter. How do those facts affect your attitudes toward abstinence?
- Why isn't oral sex safe? What would you say to someone who believes oral sex is safe?
- What changes do you need to make in your life to make abstinence part of your lifestyle?

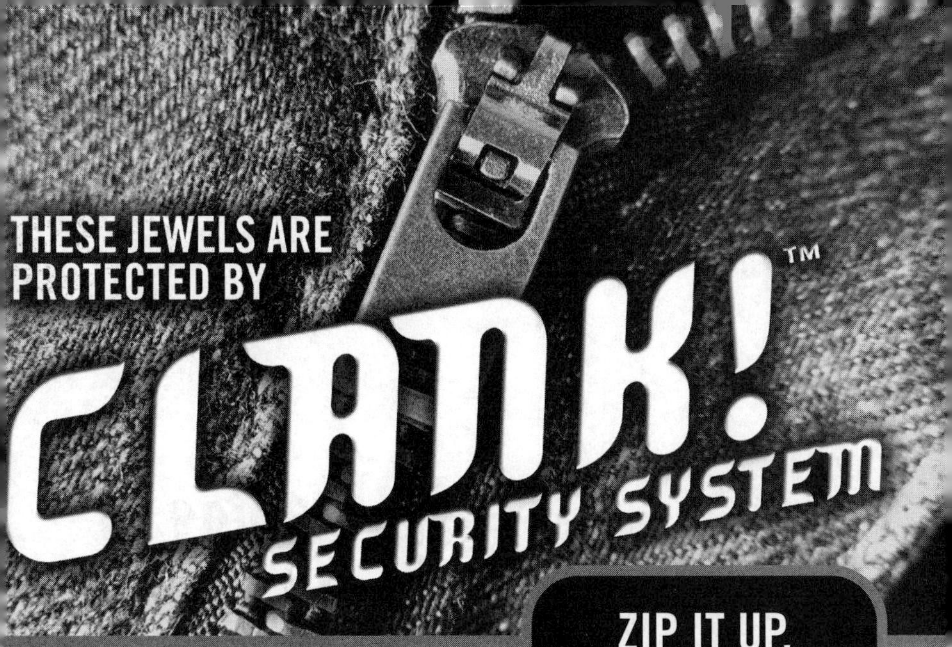
THESE JEWELS ARE
PROTECTED BY
CLANK!™
SECURITY SYSTEM

**ZIP IT UP,
LOCK IT DOWN
CLANK-CLANK!**

INSTALLATION INSTRUCTIONS

Prominently Display "Clank!"
When you subscribe to "Clank!" Security it should be apparent to your friends, to your family and to those you date, and evident in your walk, talk, dress, attitude and actions in public and behind closed doors that you are on "Clank!"

Keep Doors Closed
This means zip your pants and keep them zipped. If you prefer your doors to sag, at least pull them up over your jewels where the lock cannot be picked. Shorts and skirts should be longer than a belt, and we should not be able to read the year printed on a quarter in your back pocket. Furthermore, button up your not-see-through, correct-sized blouse over your cleavage. In other words, cover up your stuff!

Protect Yourself Against Sticky Fingers
People who own valuable possessions don't put them out for just anyone to handle with unclean hands or other parts of their body. If you don't want a disease, don't have sex with someone who has a disease. Just because they say "Hey, it's all good" and everything looks okay, don't believe them—they might be lying or they may not even know they are infected. Those who subscribe to "Clank!" require blood tests before they get married and have sex.

Limit Entrance to Those in Possession of Key
Entrance = legal marriage. Key = wedding ring. No ringy, no dingy! Until you say, "I do," zip it up, lock it down, clank-clank! All other protection systems or devices are less than 100% guaranteed!

Clank! is the only family jewel security system that insures 100% protection against Americas' Most Unwanted STDs and pregnancy.

FOR THOSE WHO DON'T WANT

itchy pus-filled scabs, bumps, warts, frothy yellow-green burning discharges, painful legions, rashes, sores, swollen testicles, infertility and maybe even death, we recommend the "Clank!" Security System.

CLANK!™ SECURITY SYSTEM

WARNING: *If you violate any of these security measures, you may deactivate "Clank!" Such breach may compromise the security system, leaving you vulnerable to any of the physical consequences of sex outside of marriage.*

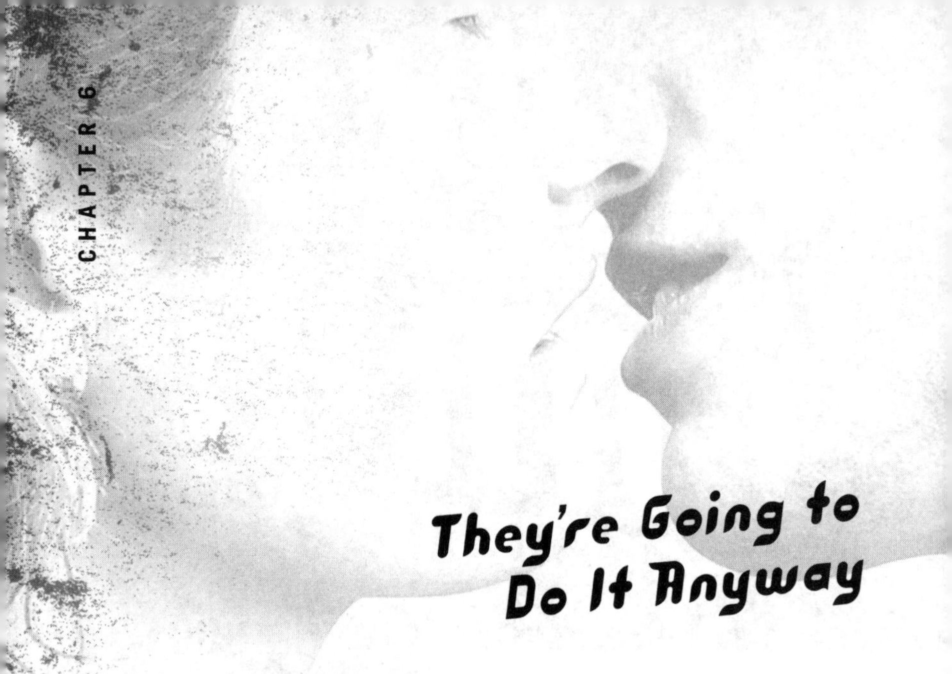

CHAPTER 6

They're Going to Do It Anyway

After I finished testifying before the Senate, I actually went across town to see a woman who helped to oversee the teen pregnancy programs across the United States. I shared my experience with her, expressing my frustration that I had asked lots of questions and not gotten any answers. For the most part, she had encountered the same brick wall, but she told me about one gentleman—a government appointee—who had responded to her questions.

She asked him, "If we know abstinence is the best thing and condom distribution is only risk-reduction at best, why do we continue to throw condoms out at these kids?"

He replied, "Oh, come on, they're going to do it anyway. Abstinence is an upper-class white value and these minority kids and poor white trash are like horny little rabbits . . . they're going to screw anyway."

I don't know about you, but it infuriates me that a government official would say this! Does this sound like somebody who respects you? Like someone who thinks highly of you? Like someone who wants to give you the best? Not at all!

> *If you've got a dream, you've got to protect it. People can't do something themselves. They tell you, You can't do it. If you want something you go get it.*—Chris Gardner (played by Will Smith) in the movie *The Pursuit of Happyness*

I take issue with this mind-set because I lived in south central Los Angeles for eight years at the height of the gang and drug wars. I don't remember anybody coming into my neighborhood and saying, "Since you're going to do it anyway, this is what we're going to do: safe drugs. I want all of you students to hold out your arms and make a fist. Now roll that sleeve up and then tie one of these rubber tubes around your arm. Okay, class . . . this is a syringe. We are going to teach you how to calculate the number of ccs of heroin you can safely inject without overdosing—because you're going to do it anyway." Have you ever heard of anything as ridiculous as this going on in a school? Of course not!

Most of you probably don't remember the race riots in Los Angeles, but I lived it! They evacuated entire neighborhoods. They had a citywide curfew. Entire blocks were burned to the ground and left without power. The National Guard was armed and posted on rooftops. In all of the chaos, I don't remember anyone coming into our neighborhood and saying, "Since you're going to do it anyway, this is what we're going to do: safe violence. We're going to make these bulletproof vests available in the nurse's office, so if at anytime you feel the urge to be violent, you can have access to as many vests as you want. Okay, class . . . we're going to go down to the firing range to teach you to become expert marksmen so that when you do your drive-bys, you won't shoot innocent babies and elderly people—because you're going to do it anyway."

Have you heard of anything as dumb as that?

"They're going to do it anyway" is a lie in truth's clothing that originates in the minds of adults and is then communicated into the lives of young people.

At a rally not long ago, I pointed out the hypocrisy by asking 6,000 high school students in attendance, "What's the legal age of drinking in this state?"

In a loud unanimous voice they yelled, "Twenty-one!"

Then I asked them to name some groups that encourage them not to drink, and they named MADD (Mothers Against Drunk Drivers) and SADD (Students Against Destructive Decisions).

I asked, "What's the legal age for smoking?"

They unanimously yelled, "Eighteen!" and said that TheTruth.com was the group that encouraged them not to smoke.

Then I asked, "What's the legal age for driving?"

"Sixteen!"

But when I asked, "What's the legal age of consent to have sex?" they began yelling out random answers: "Sixteen! Eighteen! Twenty-one!" It was mass confusion.

When I asked why they didn't know, they responded, "Because the adults haven't told us."

Why is it that for every other risky behavior, adults can send clear messages, but when it comes to common sense and sex, common sense goes out the window because common sense is not common?

No one uses this kind of doublespeak when it comes to underage drinking. MADD has been applauded for their efforts to protect the lives of America's youth, and you would never hear any sane person say to them, "You're wasting your time! These kids are going to do it anyway. Your expectations are so unrealistic—you should just teach them how to accurately calculate what amount and type of alcohol they can safely consume for their weight and sex to safely avoid the legal limit for drunkenness, just in case they should have to take a breathalyzer test."

TheTruth.com has led a very slick campaign targeted to youth, encouraging them to stop—or never to start—smoking. In their crusade against tobacco companies who market to adolescents, no one would discourage them by saying, "Why are you trying to scare these kids with the facts? You're wasting your time. They're going to light up anyway. The temptation to smoke is too great. You just need to pass out filters and teach them how to safely put them on to reduce their chances of getting lung cancer."

Yet when it comes to encouraging young people to wait for sex, abstinence educators are told that we're wasting our time. Just because not every kid will listen to the wisdom of adults doesn't mean we should lower reasonable standards. There will always be teens who smoke, drink, take drugs and even have sex, but we shouldn't lower expectations for everyone because a few choose to take risks.

Whenever I hear adults complain about the youth of today, I remind them that the kids aren't the problem—it's the adults. Not too long ago, I heard Jerry Springer (I watch him for research purposes only, of course!) make one of the most shocking statements I had ever heard on his show. I couldn't believe my ears. Twice on the same episode, he said, "Teens have no business having sex at all."

Now if Jerry Springer can get it, why can't the rest of the adult population?

If you want to see hypocrisy in action in your community, simply ask a few adults the following questions:

- Do you think minors should be allowed to drink alcohol if they want? Why or why not?
- Do you think minors should be allowed to smoke cigarettes if they want? Why or why not?
- Do you think minors should be allowed to have sex if they want? Why or why not?

The people who attach themselves to the "They're going to do it anyway" lie in truth's clothing are deceived. They usually come from one of two different camps:

"Camp A" is the adult who couldn't wait to have sex for herself. Because she didn't have any self-control or self-discipline and didn't believe in the rewards of delayed gratification, she didn't think anyone else could possibly live an abstinent lifestyle.

"Camp B" is the adult who believes that others can't possibly have the same high level of self-control and self-discipline that he has. That adult's superiority and prideful attitude is reflected in comments like the one from the government appointee from the beginning of the chapter.

These people are telling you that you don't have the capability to make—let alone follow through on—the best decisions for yourself. The Naked Truth is that you're going to have to make a decision for yourself, because the people in Camp A and Camp B aren't going to be of any help (even though they're adults).

I once heard of a study in which an average group of students was randomly divided in half. Both groups were given the same books, curriculum and assignments. Everything was the same, except for one small difference: the expectations of their teachers. The first class was told by their teacher that they were average students. The second class was told that they were brilliant and exceptional students but that their previous test scores hadn't reflected it. This class's teacher promised to work with them to make sure the students' true level of intelligence was revealed by the end of the year.

One teacher recognized average and expected average. The other teacher believed in the students, presented high standards and expectations, and committed to helping them achieve the expected standards. At the end of the study, researchers found that both sets of students believed what they were told and responded accordingly. One class far exceeded the other in performance, and you probably don't have to wonder for very long which class it was!

In my own life, I know that if I had not had parents and a few teachers who countered the general expectation of many in my community, I would have had no positive encouragement to strive for academic excellence. If I had not had a handful of individuals who told me it was possible to wait until marriage for sex—counteracting the messages of friends, music, TV and movies—I would have never heard the word "abstinence."

The Naked Truth is that abstinence as a lifestyle is the best choice when it comes to sex. Be suspicious of anyone who tries to tell you otherwise! It's never too late to start an abstinent lifestyle. Will everybody achieve the optimal goal? No. There will always be people who are going to gangbang, smoke, drink and do a lot of other risky things, including having sex. But the solution is not to remove or lower the standard, but instead to challenge, encourage and equip people to achieve their optimal goal.

Everything you hear will either pull you toward or draw you away from what you're supposed to be in life. If you're not consciously rejecting the negative things that you hear, then subconsciously you will start to internalize and meditate on them. When you start to meditate on them, you will start to believe them—and, ultimately, act on them.

Words have power. As a matter of fact, words are so powerful that Proverbs 18:21 says, "The tongue has the power of life and death, and those who love it will eat its fruit."

Words have power—both those you speak and those you hear. They will either help you develop into the person that God calls you to be, or they will distract you from it.

The Naked Truth is that you achieve what you believe.

Impressionable minds live up—or down—to the expectations placed on them. Who will you listen to? To the world? To your friends? Or to what God says about you? Will you listen to lies in truth's clothing, or will you heed The Naked Truth?

Ask Yourself

- What expectations do you have for yourself? Your friends? Your grades? Your life?
- If what you achieve is what you believe, take a moment and write three sentences about what you believe about yourself and your future.
- Why is "They're going to do it anyway" a lie in truth's clothing? What is The Naked Truth? How can you make it true for you?

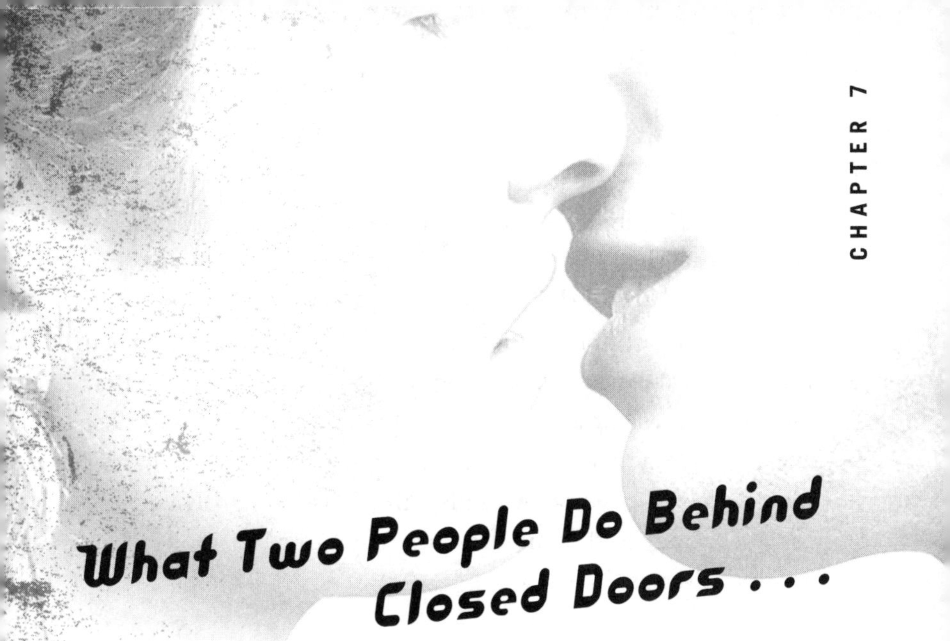

CHAPTER 7

What Two People Do Behind Closed Doors . . .

The other day I was standing in line at the grocery store behind a young teenage girl who was decked out in the latest rags from head to toe. Earrings: CoCo Chanel. Shirt: DKNY. Jacket: Phat Farm. Bracelet: Tiffany. Jeans: Rocca Wear. Shoes: the latest Nikes, straight out of the box! Her hair was laid and her nails were as freshly manicured as if she had just stepped out of the salon, rhinestones and all. Some, but certainly not all, of her threads were knock-offs. (I am the queen of knock-offs, so I would know.) I thought to myself, *Where does a teenager get money to buy such extravagant clothing?*

Her parents could be wealthy, or maybe she married early to a rich dude. But when she reached inside her Louis Vuitton bag and pulled out her food stamps, it all became clear to me. I noticed that her entire grocery basket was full of formula for her baby. I said to myself, *Either she has found a great secondhand shop or clothing bank, or I'm paying for my groceries and hers, all while she sports the latest designer wear.*

Somehow this just doesn't seem fair. Don't get me wrong, I believe in helping those who find themselves in a difficult situation (i.e., they made a mistake . . . or maybe two) or circumstances beyond their control (i.e., Hurricane Katrina). But why should I support reckless and irresponsible behavior when she has no intention of changing such a lifestyle? Why is it that I pinch pennies like a miser, search for sales as if it were the lost term paper that my whole grade depends on, and work harder than a slave to pay my own bills, bills, bills—but girlfriend can use my money and some of yours (if you have a job) to buy designer clothes?

> Direct medical costs associated with STDs in the United States are estimated at $13 billion annually.[1]

What you do behind closed doors is nobody else's business—as long as you don't get knocked up, infect other people, or come out from behind closed doors, and then demand that others pay for the consequences of your irresponsible behavior. These consequences don't just impact you, your friends and your family; they can also affect total strangers you will never meet, both financially and socially.

> **Teen parents are more likely than other teens to**
>
> - drop out of school
> - have additional out-of-wedlock children
> - change jobs
> - be on welfare
> - have mental and physical health problems[2]

Children born to teens are at increased risk for

- low birth weight
- lower cognitive scores
- school failure
- becoming teenage parents
- incarceration
- drug abuse[3]

The *Real* Notorious HIV

The news media once labeled a young New Yorker, Nushawn Williams, as "The One Man AIDS Epidemic." The 20-year-old seduced girls and young women with shopping sprees, flowers and CDs.

"He made me feel special," one of his partners confided on *The Montel Williams Show*.

It turns out that Nushawn infected at least 28 women with HIV/AIDS and may have indirectly infected as many as 53 others. One man is also believed to have been infected by one of those women. A 13-year-old became infected, and so far, six babies have been born with HIV. At last report, county health officials identified 110 individuals who had sex with either Nushawn or his partners.

Once the Chautauqua County health alert hit the community, it caused a ripple effect. More than 1,400 individuals—many of them teenagers—flocked to local clinics for testing. Dr. Neal Rzepkowski, who works at the Chautauqua County AIDS clinic, knows 9 of the 13 women infected by Nushawn Williams, and he's currently treating 5 on a regular basis.

According to Rzepkowski, two of the young women have brought in their new boyfriends for counseling. Another confided in him, however, that she had not informed her new partner that she is HIV-positive. They always used condoms. Then one day she called the doctor in tears because a condom had broken. He advised her to immediately tell her boyfriend the truth about her status—she refused. Rzepkowski recalls saying to her, "You're mad at Nushawn for having sex with you, and now you're doing the same thing!"

Dr. Jeff Birnbaum, head of the adolescent HIV clinic at King County Hospital in Nushawn Williams's hometown of Brooklyn, believes that there are thousands of people like him.[4]

When all is said and done, there may be potentially hundreds—if not thousands—of individuals put at risk of the deadly virus whose origins can be traced to Mr. Williams. Should it be any of these people's business what their partners' HIV status is at the time of intercourse? Or if they are considering having sex, is it any of their business if their partner has had sex with someone who is infected with HIV/AIDS?

My friend Tammi (who you'll hear about later) was required by law to notify her many sexual partners that she may have exposed them to Chlamydia and crabs, which are not only common but curable. Yet what about a possibly fatal virus like HIV? Should individuals be required to notify sexual partners if they have been exposed to a potentially deadly virus? In the case of Nushawn Williams, authorities knew that he was infected before it ever hit the media outlets. What did they do about it? Nothing. Because that is what the law required.

> *What about syphilis? What about tuberculosis? Why is AIDS so different, especially now that is has become a treatable condition? Why have we, because of political pressure, singled out this one disease as having special privileges?*—Geraldo Rivera[5]

In an interview, Dr. Rzepkowski responded to two questions that caught my attention:

> *Interviewer:* What is the law for partner notification? Are you allowed to contact the people possibly infected?
>
> *Dr. Rzepkowski:* A person's HIV status cannot be given over to someone without the written consent of the person being tested. I could not, if I was testing some teenager, just go out into the waiting room where their sexual partner was waiting and tell them that they were HIV positive . . . That teen would have to give me written permission to discuss it with the person. But if they were to give me the names and telephone numbers of their sexual partners, I can contact the local Health department authorities and give them the information and then they can go out and knock on their doors and say, "We have reason to believe you have been exposed to HIV through sexual contact and we recommend you get tested."
>
> *Interviewer:* When a patient tells a psychiatrist that he might murder someone, the psychiatrist is required by law to break confidentiality because another person is at risk. Shouldn't the same principle of life endangerment be applied in HIV/AIDS cases?
>
> *Dr. Rzepkowski:* The responsibility is on individuals to protect themselves, to look at every sexual partner as being potentially HIV-positive.[6]

It seems that in this instance, what you do behind closed doors is other people's business if it is a curable disease, but is nobody else's business if it is a deadly virus. Somehow that just doesn't make sense.

> *We're educating more but education does not always translate into behavioral change.* —Dr. Neal Rzepkowski[7]

Recently on a flight, I started talking to the guy next to me. He opened up about losing his wife to AIDS. They were madly in love, and they had two beautiful children. Their daughter fell ill, and they discovered that the man's wife had contracted HIV/AIDS through a blood transfusion and passed it on to both of their children. He had to watch his children and his wife die, and there was absolutely nothing he could do about it. Hearing him tell his story made me feel so powerless. What could I say to this man other than their lives were not in vain, and while it might not seem like it now, God had a purpose in this tragedy. He was very encouraged and said, "You're right. I do believe that. My wife's life and children's lives have not been lived in vain." We continued to talk about prayer, and I asked him if I could pray for him. He agreed. All the time, I didn't know who this guy was.

I got off the plane, walked down the jetway and passed by a concession stand with lots of magazines. I saw a photo on the cover that looked like the guy I had just been talking with on the plane. Looking closer, I realized it *was* the guy I had been talking with—it was Paul Michael Glaser, who portrayed Starsky in the wildly popular series *Starsky & Hutch.*

Sexual actions don't only affect the direct participants. There are innocent victims: babies. As a result of Nushawn Williams's actions, at least six babies were born HIV-positive, though only one of the babies was directly confirmed as his biological child. Innocent babies! Babies who are now casualties of the choices made by others, and this drama is played out everyday across the country and around the world.

Debbie Olson, a good friend and mentor of mine, is a retired pediatric nurse of 30 years who now teaches abstinence education because of all the damage she has seen throughout the years, particularly among young girls. She tells similar stories of innocent children damaged by others' bad choices.

"I can't tell you how heartbreaking it is to see a baby screaming in pain in an incubator with its eyes red and swollen shut because it came through the birth canal of an infected mother," she says. "What's even sadder is a mother's grief as she stands over her baby, crying, 'I'm so sorry. Mommy is so sorry. Mommy would change the past if she could.'"

I hear this same sad song when I travel overseas to Africa, where the AIDS virus has taken its highest toll. An estimated 15 million children have been left orphaned by AIDS. In many countries in Africa, it's not uncommon for a man to leave his family to find work for weeks or months at a time. While away from home, he might engage in an adulterous affair with a prostitute, only to bring his wife the gift that keeps on taking: HIV/AIDS. Their children are often born with the disease, and those who are not are soon left alone when the parents die. If they're lucky, they go to live with an elderly grandmother, who might already be raising a half dozen children. If they're unlucky, the uninfected children become orphans.

On one of my most recent trips to Tanzania, East Africa, my group was brought to tears when an eight-year-old boy begged us to return to his home to meet his six-year-old sister, hoping to find a sponsor like he had. What was so sad wasn't the fact that this eight-year-old boy was now the man of the house and that he and his sister lived alone, sleeping on the dirt floor of a mud hut. It wasn't even the fact that their only valuable possession—a cow—littered their dirt floor with dung, because it slept inside the hut at night to avoid it being stolen or attacked by wild animals. What ripped our hearts out were the graves of their parents, each marked by a cross, next to the doorway of their home. Those two precious children had to pass the graves each day, constant reminders of sadness, abandonment and death.

Why do children such as these have to suffer unnecessarily? They had no choice in the matter. Many would say, "Well, if their parents had just used condoms . . ." But by now you should know that condoms are not safe. They may be *safer*, but why would any caring person put their family at risk? How would you feel if one of your parents were to put your entire family at risk by committing adultery? Would you feel better if they said, "At least I used a condom"? Would you jeopardize the lives of your future spouse and children by gambling with your sexual behavior? If the answer is no, then the time to make a decision to never jeopardize them is not after you get married, but now.

Consider This

Whatever decisions are made in the boardroom, bedroom and even the bathroom will be revealed. People have a right to privacy, but never forget that what is done in secret will always come out into the light. Think about it:

- What if surgeons didn't wash their hands behind closed doors before performing surgery?

- Forget surgeons, what about the guy with the suspicious grin on his face at the fast-food restaurant? How would you like it if he didn't wash his hands before preparing your food?

- Pedophiles almost always commit heinous acts behind closed doors.

- Drug deals happen behind closed doors, but the transactions impact entire communities.
- The largest theft in American history, the WorldCom scam (in which hundreds of billions of dollars were stolen from countless millions of Americans, leaving many bankrupt and some destitute), was committed behind closed boardroom doors.
- Remember Nushan Williams? He had sex with each of his girlfriends behind closed doors and infected many of them with HIV. Many of them infected countless others behind closed doors, too.

> *When you have sex with someone, you are having sex with everyone they have had sex with for the last ten years, and everyone they and their partners have had sex with for the last ten years.*
> —C. Everette Koop, MD, former U.S. Surgeon General

How many people do you think it's okay to have sex with before you're married? Consider the following:

Number of Sexual Partners	Number of People Exposed
1	**1**
2	3
3	**7**
4	15
5	**31**
6	63
7	**127**
8	255
9	**511**
10	1023
11	**2047**
12	4095

Note: Data assumes that every person has *only* the same number of partners as you.

Sex Is an Uncontrollable Body Function

Before Dr. Drew, the sex doctor, there used to be a little old woman known as Dr. Ruth. She used go around and say things like, "Asking young people to control their libido is asking too much. Their libido is too strong. Sex is a natural bodily function."

Listening to that kind of logic, I can't help but think, *Diarrhea is a bodily function, too, but I wouldn't want to participate in that with anybody on a daily basis.* Dr. Ruth's argument sounds crazy, but I hear those tired old lines of reason all the time.

People talk as if sex is as uncontrollable as the beating of your heart, breathing oxygen or going to the bathroom. They talk as though if they were deprived of sex, they would die.

Let's take going to the bathroom for an example. Kids learn from an early age to control the urge to go to the bathroom. If you are reading this book, chances are everyone in your peer group, including yourself, no longer wears a diaper. By the time you entered kindergarten, you were expected to have mastery over your bladder and your bowels. And if you came to school and lost control of these functions, what happened to you? You were laughed at because all of your classmates–and some of the teachers, for that matter–thought that something was seriously wrong with you.

As necessary as it is to empty one's bladder and bowels, we still have full expectations and confidence that five-year-olds can master them. I've yet to hear about diaper distribution programs at elementary schools for those who choose not to control themselves. If a child cannot or chooses not to control himself, what do we do? We send them home until they learn, or send them to a special school.

Going to the bathroom is a bodily function so necessary that if you don't go, you can and will die. Toxins will back up into your system. Not going to the bathroom would be 100 percent fatal for all six billion people on this planet. You will die if you do not go to the bathroom. Yet we entrust five-year-olds to have mastery over this bodily function before they start kindergarten.

We have higher expectations for kindergarteners to master a function that has fatal consequences if not performed than we have for young adults with a function that is *not* fatal if not performed. I am not denying that the desire to have sex is not powerful—it is—but sex is a bodily function that is under your complete control. If you never had sex, nothing bad would happen to you. Nobody has ever died from not having sex. I have yet to read the obituary section of the newspaper where it says, "Johnny, 16, died of virginity." Yet there are young people dying everyday because they bought into the lie that they can't be expected to control their sexual urges.

Before my wedding I was asked to speak to the football team at my alma mater, the University of Southern California, on the topic of sexual abstinence. I was a cheerleader at my university, and I counted it a privilege to be invited to address my team (who happened to be national champions!) during a chapel service. I jumped in feet first on the topic of sex.

As I talked with the football players, I heard answers and comments that I hadn't anticipated. They were far more mature and took the subject of abstinence a lot more seriously than I had expected. When I asked whether or not sex was uncontrollable, one young man responded, "There are few things that are uncontrollable to a disciplined man." I wanted to bow down and kiss his feet and wipe his cleats with my hair—but I abstained. The entire team agreed that having sex is a matter of choice—sometimes a very hard one—a choice under your complete control.

Kobe Bryant, one of the NBA's biggest stars, was once the darling of the American public. He was voted "Favorite Athlete" by Nickelodeon and had endorsements from all the highest Fortune 500 companies, brands like Nike, Coke and McDonalds. The endorsements brought in more than $12 million a year, on top of his $13 million-a-year contract with the Lakers.

All of this came to a screeching halt one season when a Colorado woman accused Kobe of rape. He adamantly denied any involvement. People wondered how it could be true. After all, he was married to a wife who made most models look like mud ducks, and she had just given birth to a baby girl. When the facts came out, he admitted having sex with the woman but claimed that it was consensual. The whole trial boiled down to he-said-she-said, and all we really know is that something sexual happened.

Though the charges of rape were dropped, Kobe's sponsors weren't willing to lose money. They quickly released him from his contracts for violation of the morality clause. He lost millions a year in endorsements. Over time, Kobe will probably regain the confidence of the companies that dropped his endorsement contracts, but he will never regain his reputation. Gee, I hope the sex was good.

I asked the No. 1 college football team in the nation if they thought Kobe was able to control himself and if they could control themselves if they were offered a huge sum of money.

"Gentlemen, would you zip it up and keep it zipped until marriage for the amount of money Kobe lost in endorsements?"

"Absolutely!" they responded with enthusiasm.

Everybody wants to be a comedian, so one player piped up that he'd join a monastery for that amount. Trying to top him, his friend swore that he'd line up to be castrated for that kind of cash.

"Would you lock it down for the amount of his athletic endorsement?" I asked.

"Yes!" everyone answered.

"How about just one million dollars to keep it on 'Clank!'?"

Everyone agreed.

Our negotiations continued, and ended at a far lower number—which makes perfect sense, as they were poor college students. (When you're a starving student, 75 cents to do laundry is ample change.) But I believe the point was made: Sex is completely controllable when given the right motivation.

What is your motivation? What motivates you to do the right thing, not just in the area of sex, but overall in life? Your motivation might be money. That's an obvious choice, but The Naked Truth is that convictions based on money can't be the ultimate motivator, because the highest bidder might demand that you sell out those convictions. Perhaps money isn't your motivator—is it the respect of your peers? Approval of your friends? Whatever it is, you should know that anything apart from God will fail. If you are under His complete control, none of your actions are uncontrollable.

You *can* control your body, including the decision to have sex. Philippians 4:13 says, "I can do all things through Christ who strengthens me." Notice that the Bible doesn't say you can do "something" or "a few things" or even "most things." *You can do all things*—and that includes waiting for His best and His time.

Ask Yourself

- Why is what you do behind closed doors so important?
- In what areas are you most tempted to compromise?
- What decisions do you need to make today about the areas where you're most tempted?
- What motivates you? How healthy are your motivations?
- What decisions do you need to make to stay pure?

CHAPTER 8

It Just Happened

I can't tell you how many times I've heard, "I don't know; it just happened." Let me tell you, there's no such thing as "it just happened." Tsunamis just happen, earthquakes just happen, growing a zit in the middle of your forehead the day before you take your senior portrait just happens, but sex *never just happens.*

The Naked Truth is that sex is not an event; it's a process. There are lots of things—you know what I'm talking about—that happen before the act of intercourse, and this is where you have to draw some boundaries.

> Intimacy is the ability to be completely yourself with another person.

I'm a recent newlywed. Before I was married, I had a lot of intimate relationships with both guy friends and girlfriends. Now I'm sure as you're reading this your eyebrow just went up and a voice in the back of your head said, "Hmmmm." I know what you're thinking! Intimate relationships with your guy friends and girlfriends—*what?* We've been brainwashed to believe that "intimacy" is a dirty word, but it's not! Intimacy is the ability to be completely yourself with another person. You can freely share your hopes in life, your dreams for the future, your biggest fears and your worst failures and not be afraid that the person will laugh at you or talk about you behind your back. Instead, that person will always love you and encourage you to do what is right, even if you don't want to hear it. Intimacy and sex are not the same thing. If they were, prostitutes would be the happiest people on Earth (and getting paid for it!)—but they're not.

The sad reality is that the majority of young people I meet do not get the intimacy they need at home. As a result, they leave the house—whether they realize it or not—looking for the intimacy they desire and were created to experience. Intimacy and love are communicated from parent to child by various means, but the two primary ways are verbal affirmation and physical affection. If you're not getting affirmation and affection from your parents at home—where you should be getting it—you will search for it outside your home. Many intimacy-starved kids try to find it in other activities, hobbies, friends or the Internet . . . and some try to find it in relationships with the opposite sex.

As a girl growing up, I was constantly given verbal affirmation and physical affection from both of my parents. I knew beyond a shadow of a doubt that I was loved, cherished, supported and protected. Though I loved to hear the compliments of admiring guys—I mean, who doesn't?—I never suffered from low self-esteem or felt the pressure to compromise who I was . . . I already knew who I was! Why? My parents, through their affirmation and affection, helped me discover that who I was had nothing to do with what I could do for other people, what they thought about me, or what they could get from me.

Ron Johnson, who was both a mentor and a father figure to me, once said, "Every girl must have a man in her life, a man who wants the world for her but wants nothing from her. That first man, the one who sets the standard for every other man to measure up to, should be her father."

Ron's statement is truer than I ever could have imagined! I have found that the only man to fit this description, other than my own father, has been my one and only true love—my husband, Jeffrey.

> *My relationship with my daughter is going to affect her relationship with men for the rest of her life. Every man has dated a woman with some daddy issues . . . Sometimes I'm walking with my daughter, talking with my daughter, and I just realize that my only job in life is to keep her off the pole. They don't grade fathers, but if your daughter is a stripper, then you [messed] up.*
> —Chris Rock, *Never Scared*[1]

I don't believe this is true just for girls but for guys as well. For any guys who don't think this is such a big deal, wait until *you* have a daughter one day! If you don't do your job, verbally affirming her and showering her with lots of affection, some other guy will come along and do your job for you. Daddies not doing their jobs are one of the reasons that players can deliver the same worn-out lines and still get results. First the verbal affirmation: "Ah, baby . . . you know, you're beautiful. You're so special, you know what I'm saying? What are you waiting for, Boo . . . you know I loooooove you." Then he pours on the physical affection, running his fingers through her weave—I mean her hair—and what happens? She gives up her panties.

Boys desire affection, but girls are naturally more affectionate than boys. If you don't believe me, go to the local playground, where you will see girls holding hands with each other and skipping across the playground.

I had a slumber party not too long ago and invited a bunch of my girlfriends over. (Note: You never hear guys refer to their same-sex friends as "boyfriends." They're "my boys," "my homies," "the fellas," and so forth). We piled on top of the bed, watched TV, painted each other's toenails, and talked and laughed in the dark until we fell asleep. Guys are a whole other story. I can hear them right now: "Me and my boys are tight . . . but we ain't tight like that!" That's why you'll see guys who are the best of friends not sitting next to each other in a movie theater but skipping every other seat.

If a guy doesn't get verbal and physical affection from his parents—"Son, I love you and I'm proud of you"—along with them showing up to the ball game or music gig (on time and sober), then he's going to look for intimacy elsewhere. The first girl who verbally affirms him—"You know you're my *Papi Chulo*. You know you're the man"—will have him wrapped around her little finger.

'Cause you know what? All he hears at home is this: "You ain't nothing. You ain't never going to be nothing. Every time I turn around, all you do is get into trouble, causing problems. You are so lazy. How come you don't ever take the trash out . . . hello, don't you see it climbing up the walls? I've got to tell you two and three times. Why can't you be like your brother? Boy, you need to stop hanging around those loser friends of yours. You know what, when you grow up, you're gonna be just like your . . . daddy!"

> Why would you stay somewhere you're tolerated when you can go somewhere you're celebrated? Millions of young men and women have bought into the lie that they can find intimacy in sex.

Male or female—it doesn't matter. Both leave the house looking for intimacy they don't get at home. Many believe that they have found it in some of their friendships because of the "encouragement" they receive. But are people who encourage you to have sex really your friends?

Not telling the whole truth is still a lie in truth's clothing. Do you know what they forgot to tell you? They forgot to tell you how much you will want your virginity back after you give it away. ("Oops . . . my bad!") They forgot to mention the sick feeling you'll get in the pit of your stomach when you think you or your partner is pregnant. ("Oh, snap!") They forgot to bring up what it feels like to tell your parents you have to go to the doctor because you have become a victim of America's Most Unwanted. ("Oh yeah, I forgot about that, dude.") And they forgot to tell you about being unable to look your parents or grandparents in the eye because they can tell what's *really* been going on. ("Shoot—I forgot!")

Real intimacy, the kind that my grandparents had, can't be taught in a condom distribution program, and you won't see it on late-night BET or MTV. My grandparents' relationship was for better or for worse, for richer or for poorer, in sickness and in health, until death parted them more than 6 decades and 12 kids later. What goes into this type of relationship and what makes it last? If you were to build one, what components would be necessary?

Of the teen guys I have talked to, no one lists sex as the most important part of a relationship.

I've asked thousands of teen guys what the most important thing is in a relationship. Here are the most common answers. Rank them from 1 to 6 in importance to you:

_____Honesty
_____Communication
_____Trust
_____Respect
_____Responsibility
_____The ability to accept change

Do you know what answer I never hear? Sex. Of the many, many teen guys I have talked with, no one lists sex as the most important part of a relationship. Guys are a lot smarter than people give them credit for!

If you're in a relationship that doesn't have one or more of these things, how do you think that relationship is going to end up? Terrible! That's why these qualities are part of an essential foundation of a relationship. And that's why we need to draw some boundaries.

Recently, the media has reported the FDA's approval for the manufacture and distribution of "the morning-after pill," more accurately known as "the emergency contraception pill." If you have sex and get pregnant, you can go to your local drug store, fill a prescription and abort your baby. The good news is, I have a better pill that requires no trip to your local Walgreen's, doesn't kill an unborn baby, and is absolutely free.

It's called the night-before P.I.L., or the Physical Intimacy Line. Now, the P.I.L. has 12 steps between holding hands and sexual intercourse. Around step six, you'll find French kissing. You can imagine that there are a lot of little areas in between.

A friend of mine was a high school blue-chip athlete and had university offers from all over the country. He admitted to me that he should have been as disciplined in his sex life as he was on the basketball court. He has since adopted an abstinent lifestyle, but he had a tough wake-up call before he made that decision.

One day his girlfriend (with whom he had been having protected sex) stopped him in the quad and said, "I need to talk to you."

"I can't talk right now. I'm on my way to practice," he said.

"Well, it's kind of important."

"Girl, I gotta go. I can't talk right now."

She cut in and said, "I'm late."

Frustrated, he looked at her and said, "If you late, then you better get on to class, because I gotta go."

"I'm pregnant!" she yelled.

I guess brotha man wasn't too sharp, because when he was asked about it later, all he could say was, "I don't know. It just happened."

I hear it all the time. Sista girl or a boy like the one I just mentioned comes up to me after an assembly and says, "I don't know. It just happened." But The Naked Truth is that *it didn't just happen*. That's just a lie in truth's clothing. Their friends could tell you exactly what happened, because they watched it all unfold: "I don't know why he/she says, 'It just happened.' We all saw it coming. They were staring at each other from across the classroom":

- *Then we saw them holding hands in the lunchroom.*
- *Then he kissed her on the cheek, outside the gym.*
- *Then he was hugging her up against the lockers and stuff.*
- *Then they were beneath the bleachers. It just kept going.*

There is no way it "just happened." *Events* happen, and sex is not an event (unless you are a victim of rape). There is always some type of premeditation. Sex is a process.

That's why the P.I.L. is so important. You can go from holding hands to an arm around the shoulder to an arm around the waist to hugging to a kiss on the cheek to a peck on the lips. Once you begin French kissing, there's heavy petting . . . and you know what? You start rolling down a slippery slope, and it becomes increasingly hard to stop. So slow your roll!

That's why you have to set your boundaries. The boundary I set for myself was not just waiting until I was married before I had sex, but waiting until I was married before I kissed another guy. The next man I kissed would be my husband. I remember my last kiss before my wedding day. I was in high school, and I thought, *Okay, I have overstepped some boundaries.* The guy wasn't even my boyfriend. And I decided from that point on, up until the time I got married, I wasn't even going to kiss a guy.

When I was a single, I was often approached by interested young men. Within the first few minutes of conversation, the questions would be posed as to whether or not I was involved or available. It was never long before these men found out that I was a virgin. Some guys' eyes would light up as if they had won the lottery, and I would secretly smile to myself because I could read their twisted minds. I could tell they were thinking, *She has obviously never met a real man like me. Just give it some time and she'll be all mine.*

However, after realizing that I wasn't the stereotypical insecure, eager-to-be-accepted virgin portrayed in the movies, most would say, "It was nice meeting you" and move on. You don't have to be Dr. Phil to figure out that this quick exit in behavior was a clear sign that they weren't interested in me as a person or as a friend. Sex was a higher priority to them than friendship or any relationship of substance.

The guys who stuck around were few, but they are still my friends. A few of them could have been prospects—we had shared values, goals and interests—and because we respected each other's boundaries, none of us has any regrets. We attended and participated in each other's weddings and look forward to our kids growing up together.

Most of my friends can't say this about their past relationships. In relationships where sex was a factor, both parties feel a lot of bitterness, guilt, anger and animosity. Needless to say, these feelings would make it hard to continue the friendship. They try to avoid each other. When their paths cross, there's the inevitable "Who's that?" question from the new partner, which produces uncomfortable feelings on all sides. I can't tell you the awkwardness and drama that could have been avoided had sex not entered the picture.

When I first started talking to Jeffrey, the man who is now my husband, he had the utmost respect for my commitment to abstinence. Though he was not a virgin, he had been abstinent for quite some time and had also decided to wait until marriage for sex. But he thought I was out of my mind not to even kiss.

When I told him, he thought, *Let the negotiations begin.* Though he's a godly man, he's still a man. Now, my husband has several Ivy League degrees, and one of them is a post doctorate from Harvard in negotiations. He was very confident that his smarts and education would give him the upper hand. But on our wedding day when the minister said, "You may now kiss the bride," we kissed for the very first time. I looked my husband in the eye as I read my vows: "Before you there was no one, and there will be no one after you, Jeffrey. I loved you before I ever knew you and I saved myself just for you."

I want to make it clear that my standard not to kiss until my wedding day is not one I impose on others. There is nothing wrong with kissing. I chose this standard because of my public stand for abstinence. I was recently at a White House reception to commend the President of Uganda in his fight against AIDS, and in my speech I remarked, "I'm really tired of people saying that abstaining until marriage is unrealistic. I'm not hurting for dates and it's not because of a lack of opportunity. Not only have I waited but I didn't even kiss my husband until we said 'I do.' So if I can do it, there is no excuse for anybody else. Don't tell me it's not possible. It's very doable–you just have to choose not to do it."

Sex is not an event. It's a process. When you skip all the fun stuff of getting to know somebody, sex becomes the driving force in the relationship and you don't have a relationship anymore. It's all about the sex, and that's when people start getting hurt.

Some people say, "It just happened," but the Bible says there's a lot that goes on before it "just happens." James 1:13-15 says:

> When tempted, no one should say, "God is tempting me." For God cannot be tempted by evil, nor does he tempt anyone; but each one is tempted when, by his own evil desire, he is dragged away and enticed. Then, after desire has conceived, it gives birth to sin; and sin, when it is full-grown, gives birth to death.

The best way to steer clear of temptation is to stay away from the things you know are tempting. If you do find yourself in a bad situation, you need to flee. (And remember that "flee" does not mean rationalize, justify, hang out, kick it, or to evangelize [a.k.a missionary date], but exit quickly!)

Romans 12:1 encourages, "Therefore, I urge you, brothers, in view of God's mercy, to offer your bodies as living sacrifices, holy and pleasing to God–this is your spiritual act of worship." The problem with a living sacrifice is that it keeps crawling off the altar, which is why the Bible says we need to crucify daily, to pick up our cross to follow Him.

But what if you have already had sex . . . what do you do now? How can you tactfully and openly deal with future relationships if you choose to abstain?

I'm glad you asked, because I have a few friends I'd like you to meet.

Ask Yourself

- Why do you think so many people believe the lie in truth's clothing that "It just happened"?
- Have you received affirmation and affection from your mom and/or dad at home, or do you find yourself looking for affirmation and affection elsewhere? Why?
- Can you think of some people in your life with whom you can have healthy, intimate (non-sexual) relationships? Why or why not?
- What lines do you need to draw in your life to keep yourself sexually pure?

CHAPTER 9

I Just Listen to the Beat

I don't know if you've ever been to the back lot of a movie studio, but if you've ever been on a tour at Universal Studios, you'll know exactly what I'm talking about. It's amazing how they have almost every street from any time period just around the corner: uptown, downtown, small town, big city, western, turn of the century, and even a suburban neighborhood like Wisteria Lane on *Desperate Housewives*.

I've actually visited Wisteria Lane, and it is just as beautiful in person as it is on TV. Driving down spotless streets, past full-grown trees shading the yards of perfectly manicured lawns. Each house has its own beauty, and strolling up the walkway to one of these magnificent homes makes you wish that you lived there.

Opening the front door, I expected to see an equally impressive interior, but when I stepped through the threshold, I simultaneously exited through the back of the house. The gorgeous and immaculate house was not a home at all—it was a façade. Moreover, the back of the house was nothing more than unfinished two-by-fours surrounded by overgrown weeds, lumber and paint cans. What a letdown!

Maybe if I went into the house across the street things would be better. It's a beautiful Spanish-style hacienda. But count on it: I'd find the same dirt, debris and disappointment. Each house on the block promises to be more beautiful than the last, and each one is just as empty.

In your mind's eye, imagine that I spy a house at the end of the street, tucked in a cul-de-sac. If I wasn't looking for it, I'd miss it all together. The paint is chipping and the porch creaks when I step on it. This is not a house about which you'd ever say, "Hey, I'd like to move in there." Reluctantly, I open the door . . . and to my surprise, I find a real home! I can feel the heat from the fireplace in the cozy living room, hear the laughter of children playing upstairs, and smell something wonderful baking in the kitchen. Something tells me that this is everything I've ever dreamed of when I think of "home." In fact, this is what my friends have been looking for, too.

Now imagine it's you in this fabulous house. You can see out the window that your friends are milling around in the fake street, trying every fake door with the expectation that somehow the next fake house will be "the one"—only to walk away in utter disappointment. They have yet to find a home.

So you open that window and shout out to your friends to come on over and see what's going on, but to your surprise, they laugh at you and blow you off. Why on earth would they do that? And then you remember: The house doesn't look like what they think they want. They have chosen style over substance, thinking that external appearance is a good substitute for internal essence.

We live in a culture that values the façade of style over substance and appearance over character—a culture where fans obsess over brand names, lap up the latest trivial gossip, and celebrate celebrities whose only claim to fame is that they were once on a reality TV show.

The façade is nowhere more obvious than the world of music—particularly rap and hip-hop—where stars tout their own brands of booze and clothes while sporting $500 sneakers, designer SUVs, million-dollar cribs and enough bling to light the night sky. This lifestyle has become the gold standard of success and significance in a world fashioned by popular music. With the spinning rims and sparkling ice to blind us, it's no wonder we have become so distracted that we no longer pay attention to the substance of what is said and done in entertainment. We live in a media-saturated world with sex dripping from every TV show, movie, video game, radio single and website.

Does Media Have Power?

"If I controlled Hollywood, I could take over the world."
—Vladimir Lenin

Lenin, who was the first leader of Soviet Russia, made this statement nearly 100 years ago, back in the days when people still had to "go to the movies" to see a film—a silent, black-and-white film. Today, of course, you don't have to go to an actual movie theater, with the availability of video stores, video-on-demand and downloads to your computer or iPod.

Apparently, Lenin had good instincts. A researcher for Rand Corporation, commenting on the influence of the media, said, "Boys learn they should be relentless in pursuit of women and girls learn to view themselves as sex objects. We think that really lowers kids' inhibitions and makes them less thoughtful about sexual decisions and may influence them to make decisions they regret."[1]

"A lot of teens think that's the way they're supposed to be," added Ramsey, a teen editor for a sexual health website produced at Rutgers University. "They think that's the cool thing to do. Because it's so common, it's accepted. Teens will try to deny it, they'll say 'No, it's not the music,' but it IS the music. That has one of the biggest impacts on our lives."[2]

People often underestimate the power of music and its influence over our thoughts and actions. I often hear young people say, "Music really doesn't affect me. *I only listen to the beat.*" But does the music that you listen to inspire you to become a better, more loving, kind, intelligent, honest, self-controlled, well-spoken, patient, responsible and respectful person? Or does the music inspire ideas and actions that are the opposite of these noble traits, such as rebellion, vulgarity, irresponsibility, anger, violence, disrespect and a lack of self-control? I believe music influences more than behavior. If you think of certain music styles—such as hip-hop, country, alternative and heavy metal—specific images come to mind about the fashion, language and even the company we keep.

What type of movies, television, video games and music do you take in? How much of it has an effect on you? I couldn't care less what style you like—I'm questioning the substance of its content.

Today in America . . .

- The average teenager spends three to four hours per day watching television, and 83 percent of the programming contains some sexual content.

- Adolescents who are exposed to television with sexual content are more likely to overestimate the frequency of some sexual behaviors, have more permissive attitudes toward premarital sex, and according to one research study, initiate sexual behavior. In addition, hearing sexual talk on TV has the same effect as viewing sexual content.

- The average American youth spends one-third of each day with various forms of mass media, mostly without parental oversight.
- Forty-two percent of songs on 10 top-selling CDs in 1999 contained sexual content, 41 percent of which was "very explicit" or "pretty explicit." The impact is unknown.
- Kids and teens make up 19 percent of all U.S. Internet users. That's some 18.8 million teens and another 14.1 million children. About 73 percent of teens aged 12 to 17 and 39 percent of children aged 3 to 11 are online regularly.[3]

Television

Many have debated the power and influence of media over the behavior of the masses, but we get more information from television than virtually any other media source. According to the *Wall Street Journal*, most people watch an average of 20 hours of television per week, compared to time spent reading newspapers, magazines or books, which average about 2 to 3 hours per week.[4] There have been more studies that connect television and violence than there have been studies that connect smoking and lung cancer. And since it's sex (not violence) that is intentionally used to sell everything from toothpaste to SUVs, how much more the connection between televised sexual themes and the sexual activities of the viewers? After all, the mantra is "sex sells"—not "violence sells."

We must not forget that the primary goal of television is to attract viewers so that advertising can be sold. Broadcasting and production companies try to create programs that will attract people with money to spend so that advertisers will buy commercial spots during those programs. Commercials that air during the Super Bowl are the most expensive because the most people are watching. It's all about money. Why else would advertisers spend $2.5 million on a 30-second ad?

> "I will set nothing wicked before my eyes." —Psalm 101:3

Music

When it comes to music, a lot of people say that they only listen to the beat and that the lyrics don't really matter—but it couldn't be further from the truth. Music bypasses your consciousness and goes straight to your subconscious. It really does impact you.

> *Music had the power to produce endorphin highs . . . [to] trigger a flood of emotions and images that have the ability to instantaneously produce very powerful changes in emotional states . . . [T]ake it from a brain guy in twenty-five years of working with the brain: I still cannot effect a person's state of mind the way that one simple song can.*—Dr. Richard Pelligrino, MD[5]

From brain science to music therapy to tons of anecdotal evidence, one has to be either naive or in willful denial to ignore what we all know in our guts. As renowned musicologist David Tame observed, "Music is the language of languages. It can be said of all the arts, there is none that more powerfully moves and changes the consciousness."[6]

> *The end of all music should be the glory of God and the refreshment of the human spirit.*—Johann Sebastian Bach

Think about how much music is heard in countless clubs, concerts, cars and parties. Adolescents typically listen to 1.5 to 2.5 hours of music per day, which does not include the amount of time they are exposed to music through music videos. The more time adolescents spend listening to music with sexually degrading lyrics, the more likely they are to initiate intercourse and other sexual activities. This holds true for boys and girls as well as for whites and non-whites. Sexually degrading lyrics—many quite graphic and containing numerous obscenities—are related to changes in adolescents' sexual behavior.[7]

> *Two natures strive within my breast, The one is foul the other blest. The new I love, the old I hate. The one I feed will dominate.*
> —Betty Mays

What Does the Media Say About Sex?

Much of the "love" on television is really about sex. Some genres of television are nearly completely sex-centered: soap operas, TV movies and talk shows focus much of their attention on sex-related subjects. Even though the sexual content of some shows is talk rather than portrayal of sexual behavior, the messages do not usually distinguish between marital and extramarital sex, and the morality of sexual behavior is rarely—if ever—discussed.

Love has been reduced to cheap and fleeting emotions fueled by hype and hormones. Women are treated as little more than sexual objects to be handled, sold, consumed and pimped. And the women go right along! They justify it by saying they are "keeping it real," when they are really just keeping it raunchy.

Godly love, in contrast to what you see on TV, is a love that never seeks its own good, but instead is focused on the other person. It is a love that always hopes for the best in others without seeking something in return, and it always seeks to benefit the person who is loved.

The sexual behavior depicted on television and in movies is completely irresponsible and unrealistic, and it communicates that sex is common and without consequence or commitment. Here are a few lies:

Everybody's Doing It—and If You're Not, You're Weird

The author of the book *God's Vision or Television* wrote this: "It is easy to be convinced that 'everybody is doing it' from one television show or newscast, when in fact nobody is doing it but the people on the show. The founders of MTV, for example, were very explicit in defining their aim as shifting youth culture, not just reflecting it or marketing to it."[8]

The Best Sex Is Casual and in Uncommitted Relationships

A cruel irony of hip-hop music is that many artists who have been fortunate enough to escape the poverty of the inner city—a poverty in large part fueled by cycles of fatherlessness and illegitimacy—have gotten rich singing about full-throttle sexual immorality. The media clearly portrays the image that the best sex is to be had in an uncommitted relationship. The next time you watch TV note how much sex is portrayed and who it's portrayed by—you'll be surprised at the number of couples engaging in sexual activities outside of marriage.

You Can Have Sex Without Consequences

Just how many women has James Bond slept with, anyway? What are his odds of being dead, not from some stray bullet or explosive device, but from his casual sex?

Or what about Sarah Jessica Parker? It's a good thing that *Sex in the City* ended, because they'd be hard-pressed not to have to deal with some real consequences of her promiscuity. Her character, Carrie Bradshaw, was a cat with nine lives—she was long overdue to pay the piper, so to speak!

Or check out *General Hospital*, one of the longest-running and most popular soap operas of all time. Think about it: The show takes place *in a hospital*. How is it that in America, 80 percent of reported viral infections are STDs and abortions are the most common surgical procedure after cesarean sections, but we don't see these on *General Hospital*?

What Do Celebrities Say About Sex?

Many onstage artists simulate everything from masturbation to bondage-oriented sex with band or audience members. Remember the Destiny's Child (who were professing Christians) lap dance performance several years ago? Christina Aguilera, Foxy Brown, Faith Evans, Britney Spears, Beyoncé and Jessica Simpson were all professing Christians at one time or another—one of these artists even made the cover of *Rolling Stone* wearing only her underwear, under the headline "Christian of the Year."

Female artists are often exploited. If you didn't know any better, you'd think some of these videos were *God's Girls Gone Wild.*

> *We're bored with the concept of right and wrong.*—Madonna, during the performance of "Like a Virgin" at the 2003 MTV Music Awards, during which she infamously kissed Britney Spears and Christina Aguilera

The recording artist, Snoop Dogg has turned away from gangbanging to God. When asked how he justifies his dirty mouth, porn involvement and violent themes, he says, "We keep God in everything we do, and we try to be more positive than negative."[9]

> Would you lie to me?
> Never
> Would you die for me?
> Whenever
> —Snoop Dog, "Bo$$ Playa" featuring Arch Bishop Don Magic Juan[10]

I don't know what god Snoop's worshiping, but the Bible is clear that those who love God will keep His commandments, and that blessing and cursing cannot come out of the same mouth. Media will allow anyone to profess their faith in God or even Christ as long as it fits their idea of what "god" should be.

Just pay attention to the latest awards show and watch how many "artists" come up to the microphone—in outfits made from less cotton than in an Aspirin bottle—to thank God for their latest booty-shaking video.

> *It [is] rather ironic that teenage girls with breast implants and rappers with violent and misogynistic lyrics spent the whole night thanking Jesus Christ of all people. It's clearly by unchristian means that these alleged 'friends of God' have made their millions.*—Marilyn Manson[11]

Media Imperialism

American television has an influence not just in the U.S. but also around the world. Some of my foreign friends refer to the inescapable presence of American shows as "media imperialism."

A mentor of mine returned from an advisory trip to the nation of India and shared the far reach of the media's influence. In India's recent history, it has experienced a sharp increase in its unwed teen pregnancy rate. The Indian government was baffled about what could have triggered this increase in the population. What on earth could have caused this increase of out-of-wedlock births, when everyday society seemed to be the same as before? There had been no sweeping cultural change such as the mass return of American men after WWII (igniting the "baby boom") or the sexual revolution of the 1960s.

After doing some research, the government found the common thread: Only the villages that had television sets had an increase in illegitimate births. Many of these villages had acquired a single TV for the entire community and established it in its own hut, similar to a movie theater. In some cases, the youth in the villages commandeered the huts, where only two stations could receive clear reception: BBC News and MTV. Suddenly they were watching the spanking-est new music videos. To say hormones were ignited would be an understatement. I'm sure you can figure out the rest of the story.

> *This is what I feel about a lot of the music industry. I think nobody is telling these kids the truth. That it just isn't about the bling, the perpetuation of violence, and marginalization of women, and I feel like we've just lost it and they're projecting this image around the world a superficial idea of what it's like to be successful.*—Oprah[12]

A Potential for Good

Hip-hop is the universal language among youth around the world, and I believe it has great potential for good. Its origins are found with the African-American and Puerto Rican youth of the inner city of New York, but it has gone global. Regardless of your feelings toward hip-hop, it has become the language of youth around the world.

If you don't believe me, listen to this: My friend Bradley Rapier leads a hip-hop/break dance group called The Groovaloos who took first place at the American Street Dance Championships. (If you have seen a Sprite or an iPod commercial, the movie *You Got Served*, the back-up dancers for Justin Timberlake or most any major awards show, you have seen The Groovaloos.) Bradley came back from an international dance battle and told me some of the best break dancers are from Denmark. *Denmark?!*

> *I love rap music, but I'm tired of defending it! It's hard to defend [lyrics like], 'I got hos in different area codes.' It's hard to defend 'Move, b - - - h, get out the way.' You go to the clubs and you see girls dancing, just loving it. I feel sorry for the guys that got to pick a wife out of this bunch . . . [W]omen who like rap don't care what they are saying. If the beats are right she will dance all night. I see girls on the floor dancing to the nastiest [lyrics] ever made . . . And you know what's real wild? If you mention to a woman that the song is disgusting and misogynistic, they all give you the same answer: 'He ain't talkin' 'bout me.'*
>
> —Chris Rock[13]

Still don't believe me? The brother of a friend of mine came from Austria to visit us in Los Angeles. Laurent was on a mission to bring back the 411 on the hip-hop scene. He had me driving into areas of Watts that I just don't normally go to take photos of The Watts Towers, graffiti murals and hole-in-the-wall urban gear shops, all for his latest underground remix. Laurent—who looked like an Aryan recruit for Hitler Youth but sported a fade with the best of them—couldn't wait to get back to Austria with photos of his "new girlfriend." (That would be me, I guess.) To have a girlfriend who even remotely looked like Beyoncé was a symbol of prestige.

And if that doesn't convince you that hip-hop is the international language of youth, let me tell you this: Hip-hop has also scaled the Great Wall of China. My girlfriend Amy was a TV music VJ in Hong Kong. She called to tell me that "ghetto" is all the rage in China: saggy pants, oversized American Athletic Apparel, French braids (which don't come from France, by the way), and so forth.

Recently I received a call from an Indian gentleman with an invitation for Club Varsity (the company and ministry I lead) to go to India with the abstinence message in "an authentic hip-hop production." He placed heavy emphasis on the word *authentic* because hip-hop has become so natural among Indian youth that they can sniff out wannabees. Though India literally has dozens of languages and dialects spoken around the country, this Indian man was so excited at the prospect of Christians coming to India to speak "the language of the youth."

You may prefer other forms of music and dress, but Garth Brooks doesn't pull this kind of weight around the globe. The universality of hip-hop music and culture is unlike anything the world has ever seen.

It is not only hip-hop that has the potential for good. Any form of media, used to communicate in a coordinated fashion, can elicit change. In Uganda, as we saw in earlier chapters, the entire nation banded together to promote the primary message of abstinence. The message was delivered in middle school classrooms, churches and community events through radio, print and television broadcasts. The government established highly effective partnerships with the religious community, working cooperatively to design and implement the ABc program. The effect was to create what researchers call a "social vaccine" against HIV: a set of cultural values that encourage more responsible sexual attitudes and behaviors.[14]

Media—including TV, movies, music, video games and the Internet—is neither fundamentally good nor ultimately evil. It's the *messages* contained in the media that are moral or immoral, and you must be alert and become aware of those messages so that they do not influence your decisions without your permission. Media can be a fun and effective way to communicate—I'd be quite the hypocrite if I said I was anti-media!—but you have to be smart . . . don't "just listen to the beat." Listen to God's Word: "A false witness will perish, and whoever listens to him will be destroyed forever" (Prov. 21:28). When the media is telling lies in truth's clothing, don't listen to the beat! Turn it off—or better yet, make your own media and join me in telling The Naked Truth.

Ask Yourself

- What type of movies, television, video games and music do you take in? How much of it has an effect on you?
- In what ways are you just listening to the beat right now in your own life?
- What changes do you need to make in your own life with regard to the types and quality of media you watch and listen to?

CHAPTER 10

Peer Pressure/ Everybody's Doing It

This next lie in truth's clothing is probably the most potent, the most powerful and the most deceptive of them all. Why? Because it's the number one reason teens give when asked why they get involved with sex, drugs, alcohol, violence and every other risky behavior. This lie is so diabolical and has such a grip on the minds of American youth that not a week goes by that you're not indoctrinated with this lie. The lie is peer pressure.

The Naked Truth is that there is no such thing as peer pressure. Peer pressure is a media creation—like Britney Spears. It's a lie because what you see and what you hear is not what's really going on. It's only made to look more impressive than it really is. The reality is that if you show me your friends, I will show you your future. This is why you have to really be conscious all the time of decision-making skill No. 3: "Find other people who will support your decision."

A few years ago, I was filming a Fanta soft drink commercial with this unknown-at-the-time model named Tyra Banks. Now, the way you film a party scene is to get dozens and dozens of people on a sound stage, which is a big huge open room where sound travels. So we're filming the scene, dancing with these Fanta soft drink cans when the director says, "Cut, everybody take a break on the set."

We all started to chill out, sitting up against the walls and in little groups on the floor. I went off to the side to read my book, minding my own business. I was not trying to dig into anyone's trail mix if you know what I'm saying.

Out of the blue, a girl turns around from a huddle of girls and demands in her breathy, I'm-too-sexy-for-you voice: "So, Lakita . . . tell me about your sex life."

I said, "Excuse me, but I don't have a sex life."

She tossed her hair over her shoulder and replied, "Well, tell me about your last sexual experience."

I tossed my hair back at her and said, "I don't have a last sexual experience."

You might have thought I just talked about her momma, because her eyes popped wide open, her jaw dropped and hit the floor and she screamed, "You mean you're a virgin?!"

Of course she said it so loud that everyone in the room heard. At that moment, my whole life turned to slow motion. I could see people turning around, gasping as they pointed at me, turning to whisper to their friends and, yes—I think I even saw a few choke on their own spit. But did she stop? Noooooo, she kept right on talking. "Oh my God, I mean I can't believe all the guys you haven't been with, all the things you haven't done, I mean, don't you feel like you're missing out on anything?"

It felt like time stopped. It was the longest pause in the space-time continuum. No one had ever put me on the spot like that.

I'm not going to lie to you: The pressure was great, and the first thing that came to my mind was *I can't believe she's clowning me in front of all of these people.* But this was the moment of truth. I had to be honest and bare my soul because she had just undressed me in front of everybody and their momma.

I looked over and said, "You know, you're right. I have missed out. I have missed out on the thrill of waking up wondering if my early pregnancy test will turn blue. I missed out on not getting to walk into a clinic with my best friend holding my hand because my boyfriend isn't going with me unless he's dragging me in. I missed out on sharing the same joy as my ex-roommate, who has pinpointed the day her child would have been born if she had not aborted, and who cries herself to sleep every year because she's named him and celebrates his birthday. I'm even more saddened that five years from now I'll miss out on waking up to stare at the ceiling of an AIDS hospice like my cousin Ricky and my friend Rod before they died. Rod was quite the man. He used to mock me relentlessly about being a virgin. 'Girlfriend, come on–you just need to practice and teach safe sex. I mean, they're going to do it anyway. Why are you wasting your time? Everybody's doing it!' But Rod didn't laugh anymore, not when he withered away to less than 100 pounds, with his eyes sunk back in his head. You could literally smell the stench of rotting flesh before you got to his room because of the open sores and boils all over his body. He didn't laugh when I had to wait outside his door while the cute orderly came in every hour on the hour to change his diaper because he had diarrhea 80-something times a day."

I looked over at girlfriend that day and said, "You're right. I have missed out . . . on all the wonderful opportunities you've opened yourselves up for."

And the room went silent.

Before he died, Rod told me to never forget what I saw so that I could recount it to anyone who would listen. He begged me never to stop talking about the abstinence lifestyle and said that if he had a little sister he would tell her to do exactly what I was doing. The biggest shock came when he revealed that all along, he had secretly hoped I would make it to the altar as a virgin, even when he was hassling me about it. Rod came to a moment of truth: He admitted to himself and to me that our friendship kept reminding him that what he was doing wasn't right.

This encounter led me to wonder, why do people try to get you to do things that you know are wrong, that *you* know *they* know are wrong, and that *they* know *you* know *they* know are wrong?

"Let's just try some of this weed, man."

"Let's cut class, 'cause you can turn your homework in tomorrow."

"Your parents aren't home, so they'll never find out."

Whenever you find yourself pressured in these or similar situations, realize first that what you are being encouraged to do is probably something you shouldn't be doing in the first place. (How often do you get pressure from your friends like "Just try some of this wheat grass, man" or "Let's stay after class and see if we could do some extra credit" or "Your parents aren't home, so let's clean up the kitchen and take out the trash before they get back"? Pa-lease!)

Realize second that these are not your friends.

We like to blame everything on peer pressure, but let's just call it like it is: Misery loves company. When people are livin' foul, they make themselves feel better by getting others to participate with them. Then, if they should get caught, they can dress up their actions by saying, "Hey . . . *everybody's doing it.*"

I've heard this many times and I always respond, "Then you'll have no problem finding somebody else to do it, because I am not Everybody." Since when did the agreement of a majority make something right—anybody remember a little thing called slavery? Or the Holocaust?

The Naked Truth is that misery loves company.

That day filming the Fanta commercial, a thought dawned on me: People are just like the soda cans. What happens when you squeeze an empty soda can? It gets crushed. Why? Because the pressure on the outside of the can is greater than the pressure on the inside. The inverse is true as well. What happens when you squeeze a full soda can that's still sealed on top? It can't be crushed. Why? Because the pressure on the inside of the can is greater than the pressure on the outside.

The problem with our culture is that people use peer pressure as an excuse for bad behavior when in fact they are simply empty of any true substance. Whenever they are subjected to any pressure from the wrong people to do the wrong thing at the wrong time in the wrong place, they collapse. Peer pressure is nothing more than a lack of character.

Building Character

Character: a distinctive trait, a behavior typical of a person or group, moral strength

The origins of the word "character" come from the Greek word *charassein,* which means "to engrave, to chisel with pressure and heat"—like a statue carved in stone or cast in bronze.

A Portrait of Character

Have you seen the Statue of Liberty? She is the best illustration of the idea of "character" that I know. As you envision her, think about where she is. What does she look like? How did she look 50 years ago? How will she look tonight, tomorrow, the next day, next year?

Guess what? She never changes. That's character. Rain, snow, the sun beating down, birds dropping love notes—or even you standing at the bottom and yelling obscenities at her: None of these things matter. She will never change. That's character. Character is what you are when nobody else is looking.

* * *

When the immigrants came in mass-migration from Europe over 100 years ago, many were brought to tears when they saw the statue of Liberty because she was exactly as she had been described to them. She was exactly as they had seen her pictures or drawings. She lived up to her reputation—in other words, her character matched her reputation.

Reputation is what others say about you, whereas character is *what you are.* Maybe you don't like your reputation. Maybe you don't *have* a reputation. Whatever the case, if you don't like your rep, change your character—and let the chips of your reputation fall where they may. Remember, it's your character—not your reputation—that will determine who you will be in the future.

* * *

So how does a master craftsman create an imposing character like the Statue of Liberty?

He has a vision that no one else can see. He takes an indistinguishable lump of nothing—that no one else thinks is worth anything—and begins to apply pressure and heat and time and sweat. He doesn't give up until what He has created matches His vision, until the character standing before Him is exactly what He intended him or her to be.

Are you ready to be crafted into a person of character, a work of art in the hands of the Master Craftsman?

Character is impervious to all external forces, except those that will help mold it into what it was created to be. That's why it is so important to surround yourself with people who will support your decisions. Seek people out who are living a life worthy of imitating. Find people who are excellent at something. Their influence will help shape you into the character you are meant to be.

What Is Character?

- It is your personal conviction.
- It empowers you to resist outside pressure from media and peers.
- It is reinforced by the company you keep.

What Is *Your* Character?

- When your parents aren't home . . .
- When your friends are around . . .
- When you're with your girlfriend or boyfriend . . .

What's right is not always popular and what's popular is not always right. And that is The Naked Truth.

I was reading the Bible this morning and came across a verse that says "Bad company corrupts good character" (1 Cor. 15:33). If you hang out with bad company, your good character *will* be corrupted. Of course, it would be impossible for you to never associate with individuals with "bad" behavior, but "keeping company" is an entirely different story. Compromise doesn't happen overnight; it happens a little bit at a time.

But do you know what's really interesting? I was reading earlier in Romans 1, which is a whole chapter about the depravity of mankind. At the end of the chapter, verse 32 says, "Although they know God's righteous decree that those who do such things deserve death, they not only continue to do these very things but also approve of those who practice them." In other words, people who participate in doing evil like to encourage others to do it with them—a perfect illustration of misery loves company.

> What's right is not always popular and what's popular is not always right.

If your top priority is your relationship with God and He is the one from whom you seek approval, the only real pressure that will affect you will come from Him through the Holy Spirit. By following Him, you won't find yourself in compromising situations—but even if you do, He will provide a way out!

One of the first things the Holy Spirit told me just after I became a Christian as a teenager was "You will be seen by the eyes of millions, but you must perform for an audience of One." God is my audience of One. When you're focused on God and what He thinks about you, it won't matter what kind of pressure others try to put on you. You truly couldn't care less! Remember the Scripture, "He that is in me is greater than he that is in the world" (1 John 4:4).

Ask Yourself

- Do you think peer pressure is real? Why or why not?
- What is character? How would you describe your character? What is reputation? How would you describe your reputation?
- Who in your life most tempts you to do things you shouldn't? What is stopping you from removing yourself from this person's influence?
- What changes do you need to make in your life in order to live for an audience of One?
- Read Daniel 1. How did Daniel and his friends deal with pressure?

CHAPTER 11

It's Too Late For Me

If the truth will make you free, how much more will a lie keep you in bondage? Less than half of all American high school students have had sex by the time they graduate, but two-thirds of those wish they had waited.[1]

One of the most frequently heard and hardest lies to be set free from is "Knowing what I know now, if I had to do it all over again, I'd still be a virgin . . . but I've already done it, so *it's too late for me*." This is one lie in truth's clothing that keeps many of your friends (and maybe even you) from one of the most important decisions you will ever make.

If you hear that voice in the back of your head saying, "There is no way I can start all over again—are you kidding? What will my friends think and what am I going to tell them?" . . . you are not alone. I don't care what you've done before—what you did, where you did it, how you did it, how many times you did it, with whom and how many people you did it—I care about the decisions you're going to make *today*, and what you're going to do with those decisions from now until you say "I do."

The Naked Truth is that it's never too late to start making the right decisions. Granted, you will never be able to get your virginity back physically, but you can regain it emotionally, psychologically, relationally and spiritually.

The Naked Truth is that it's never too late to start making the right decisions.

If you've already engaged in sexual activity, there are a couple of things that you need to do if you want to live an abstinent lifestyle. The first is to stop having sex. Hello! I know that sounds really obvious, but it's better to state the obvious than be unclear.

Weaning yourself off of sex is ridiculous. It won't work. Clearly, more than one person is involved in sex, so you need to be prepared for the reaction of that special someone when you break it to them that you've decided to lock up the goods. Decide now that you'll go cold turkey no matter the response from your significant other, because I guarantee that tapering off is about as effective as "I'll start my diet tomorrow." *You* have to make the decision to stop having sex—getting a consensus on the matter will most likely end in frustration. The person you've been having sex with will probably react in one of three ways:

1. *I just don't see how we can be together, so . . . see ya.* Of course this will come after they give you some feeble attempt to talk you out of your decision, but ultimately they will be gone—and without the goodies. As long as you don't compromise, this person will expose himself or herself for who he or she really is. After all is said and done, you'll know that what he or she wanted most was sex, not genuine friendship.

2. *A challenge! This is going to be fun.* This person may try to seduce you with an array of different tactics—from outright seduction to guilt and manipulation, such as, "Why is sex such a big deal all of the sudden?" or "If you really love me you wouldn't do this to our relationship." Blah, blah, blah, blah. Stay strong. No ringy, no dingy.

3. But if the person really loves you and values your friendship, he or she will respect your decision and support you in this new transition. Surprisingly enough, the other party is often relieved because he or she desired the same thing deep down inside but was afraid to share it. Both individuals often find that their relationship becomes deeper and more transparent once sex is eliminated from the equation.

Once you make the decision to live an abstinent lifestyle, you need to start looking at the people you're hanging with and decide whether or not these base creatures are really your friends. What is their conversation like? What is their attitude toward sex? How do they feel about abstinence? You probably already know the answer to these questions. If you know they have your back, these are true friends. If not, you have to start making new friends who have the same values and goals that you have adopted. After all, you will become the company you keep. As my grandmother used to say, "Birds of a feather . . ." Well, you know the rest.

The Naked Truth is that good decisions for the future do not erase the bad consequences of the past.

After you make the decision to stop having sex, the second thing you need to do is *get tested*! The Naked Truth is that good decisions for the future do not erase the bad consequences of the past. In getting tested, you may find out that you are pregnant or have a sexually transmitted disease. (By the way, if you test negative for STDs, you need to get tested again at a later date, because many STDs—like HIV—may not show up until much later, even if you have been abstinent.) If you have been victimized by some of America's Most Unwanted, it's not the end of the world. Many STDs are curable, and there are treatments available for the ones that aren't that can help you live a full and healthy abstinent lifestyle.

The third thing you need to do is start making better decisions. This starts with setting up boundaries, as we discussed earlier. Make a plan for what you will do if you find yourself in a difficult situation. If you want to use your family as an excuse, do it. Until I was older and bolder in my convictions, I always used my mother and brothers as my reason to say no. I had four extremely large older brothers—all over six feet and more than 200 pounds each—and a mother who carried a gun in her purse, fo' real! I had fun thinking up crazy scenarios about what they would do to anyone who even suggested something out of line, and then shared those mental pictures with anyone who tried to pressure me. (And really, anything I could dream up wasn't too far outside the realm of possibility.)

Some things are just common sense. I have come to believe that common sense is not very common, but there are a few things that everybody needs to figure out. Let me give you a common sense heads up:

Thinking about having a guest over when your parents aren't home, particularly a guest of the opposite sex? Not! Everybody knows that the couch has a horizontal gravitational pull—it's scientific.

Or maybe your parents *are* home, but your guest has been escorted to your bedroom with the door closed. Have you lost your mind? This goes back to the issue of character and what you do behind closed doors. My momma once told me, "Never let yourself be caught in a conversation or situation that you wouldn't want to be interrupted in."

My momma once told me, Never let yourself be caught in a conversation or situation that you wouldn't want to be interrupted in.

How about this oldie but goodie: curfew. I used to hear my aunt tell my cousin (as she was on her way out the door on a date) to be home on time "because there is nothing open after midnight except for legs." (I think I was 13 when I figured out what this meant.) When I was living at home, my parents set my curfew according to my age:

- Elementary school: Be inside when the street lights come on.
- Middle school: You best be in by 9 P.M.
- High school: In before 10 on a school night, 11 on weekends, and if there's a school-sanctioned event (like prom), then we'll negotiate.

When I went away to college, I realized that I could finally set my own curfew. But wouldn't you know—when you train a child in the way she should go, she doesn't depart from it. At least I didn't. My roommate and I set and enforced our own curfew. We decided that if we had male friends over, they had to be gone by a certain time, and we had a code for the other to ask our guest to leave if he didn't get the hint the first time. There are certain boundaries that you must draw if you want to make good decisions.

Living a New Life of Abstinence

You may still believe that once you've crossed the line, it's unrealistic to turn back. If so, I'd like to reintroduce you to a few friends of mine, friends that you met in previous chapters. I knew some of them before they made the decision to abstain, and I met some of them after they were already living the abstinent lifestyle. But I'll tell you this: When I hear them share their stories about their lives before making this decision . . . I kid you not, I always think they must be talking about somebody else! They have transformed into entirely different people. But don't take my word for it—you can decide for yourself:

Remember Barb from Chapter Two?

Barb was about to get married when she decided to get tested for STDs to put her mind at ease. That's when she found out she was HIV-positive and had between two weeks and one year to live.

When she tearfully told her husband-to-be the news, he said, "I have already committed in my heart to marrying you, and I will not go back on that commitment." That was in 1993. In the fall of 2003, Rick and Barb Wise celebrated their tenth wedding anniversary. Though they maintain some sexual restrictions (one being that they do not have children), they continue to enjoy a great life together.

Remember Luis from Chapter Five?

By the age of 29, Luis had three kids with three different women, had killed two babies through abortion and was paying child support. That's when he knew he had to change.

One afternoon in his apartment, something came over him. "I didn't know what it was in that moment, but looking back now, I know it was the Holy Spirit," Luis says.

> I decided to say, Lord forgive me. Whatever I need to do, I'll do it, but help me. I grabbed a Bible that was sitting nearby and it opened to Galatians 5, which talks about the fruit of the Spirit. I read the words "Those that practice such things will not inherit the kingdom of God." I got scared. Then I started praying more, crying more, and then opened the Bible again, this time to Deuteronomy 28, which talks about the things that happen when you do good and the things that happen when you do bad. So I closed the Bible again and cried and prayed some more, and then opened it to Ecclesiastes 9:7, which says, "Go, eat your food with gladness, and drink your wine with a joyful heart, for it is now that God favors what you do." And I did. I went to sleep in peace, and I started going to church every day.
>
> Eventually, I had the invitation to become an abstinence speaker. Through the experience, I realized how low I had gotten, but on the other hand, how great is our God.

And Do You Remember Tammi from Chapter Nine?

After being raped by a stranger at 15 years old, Tammi began partying and dating and sleeping with every guy she met, hoping for a real relationship. Eventually, she contracted an STD and became suicidal. In college, she hit rock bottom.

Well, the story doesn't end there. She says, "I remember going back to my dorm room and sitting on the edge of my bed and thinking, 'Is this my life? I have not achieved my goals; I have an STD and a bad reputation. I want things to change.' I remembered a woman I had met who had invited me to a Bible study. The topic that night was on sex and dating from a Christian perspective. That's where I learned that the Bible says to wait for marriage to have sex, and even if you have had sex you can choose secondary virginity. I knew I needed this." Tammi goes on:

> At 22, I began to practice a life of abstinence, and I began to see who I really was. I started to put my best foot forward. On dates, we'd go out for a pizza and movie and maybe hold hands. Not only was it fun, but at the end of the night you felt good about yourself, instead of trashy, used or abused. And guess what—they call you again! I ended up meeting my husband when I was 26, and though he had had sex in the past, he was abstinent for six years before we got married.
>
> It was exciting to meet my husband and practice abstinence. He fell in love with *me*. Holding hands was exciting. Kissing was exciting. Having sex after we were married was exciting. And the whole time, I was confident that he fell in love with *me*, just me, everything about me—my quirks, my faults, the good things about me—and that brought confidence to me. I regained my self-respect, my dignity, my usefulness and the joy that I had lost in the past. Had I not chosen abstinence, I don't think I would have met my husband. I don't think I would be the person I am today, the person who knows who she is, has self respect, has dignity and can walk around with my head held high.
>
> The choice to practice secondary virginity was a turning point for me. I feel like if I hadn't done that, I would have continued to have premarital sex and possibly get more sexually transmitted diseases. I could have contracted AIDS or gotten pregnant. I'm scared to think of the way I would be if I hadn't turned my life around at that point.

> My life today is fabulous in so many different ways, and a lot of it is because of the choice I made when I was 22. I've been married for nine years, and we have four children. I'm confident that my husband loves me no matter what, no matter what I look like, no matter what we're going through. The truth is that there's more to life than just sex. We're happily married, our kids are wonderful, and it's greatly due to my decision to choose abstinence that I can be as confident as I am.

The person with an argument is always at the mercy of the person with an experience—especially an experience that has produced change. Those are my friends!

Many have said that to wait until marriage for sex is unrealistic and impossible . . . but I did it. In much the same way, my friends are a testament that it is never too late to start making good decisions. They didn't sugarcoat the past, gloss it over, justify it or glamorize it to make themselves look good. They called it what it was (sin), they repented of it and they chose to live healthy, good and worthy lives. They found the strength, courage and wisdom to break free from the father of lies and found The Naked Truth. Won't you consider breaking your bonds and running for freedom?

Ask Yourself

- Are there any areas in your life where you're buying into the lie that "It's too late for me"?
- What changes do you need to make in your life to embrace The Naked Truth that it's never too late for you?
- Who do you know that needs to hear the truth that it's not too late? What's stopping you from speaking those words into someone else's life?

CHAPTER 12

Marriage Is Just a Piece of Paper

My little sister, Lauren, is a phenomenal singer. Okay, she's not my sister. But she is an amazing singer and songwriter. We're a lot like sisters—she borrows my clothes, we share lots of meals together, and we love to hang out. You may have heard her voice and not realized it, especially if you've ever heard the Cheetah Girls or The Bratz. Lauren and I have traveled together around the world doing concerts (for those of you who don't know, I'm a rapper) and speaking to countless millions of young people about abstinence. She's living the abstinent lifestyle and waiting for Mr. Right instead of settling for Mr. Right Now.

Lauren called me over the holidays just to holla at a sista. She said her grandfather, John, had moved in with her family. It was the first Christmas he's been apart from his wife and it was taking a toll on everyone. The really hard thing was listening to her grandfather talk as if her grandmother, Mildred, was still alive. John was finding it difficult to be alone for the first time in more than 50 years.

Lauren shared their story with me. As a young girl, Mildred volunteered to write letters to the men in her church denomination who were serving overseas in the military during WWII. She befriended a young soldier with whom she became close pen-pals, and she was heartbroken to receive the notice that he had been killed in combat.

As sad as she felt, Mildred knew his family was grieving even more. She began writing letters to console the soldier's family, and through this tragic event, she met the soldier's younger brother, John. They quickly became good friends and wrote each other often, and as time passed they began to sense that this friendship could be more than just a pen-pal relationship. Though they had never even spoken on the phone, Mildred and John fell in love.

Keeping it to herself and praying to God for direction, Mildred continued to write to John as usual, until one day she received a letter that read, "If you can tell me the verses in the Bible that God has put on my heart, I will know that He has chosen you to be my wife."

With more than 31,000 verses in the Bible, Mildred knew it was impossible without God's help. It would be like trying to find a needle in a haystack or locating one star at random from our entire galaxy. But Mildred wrote John back and quoted Ruth 1:16-17: "Where you go, I will go, and where you stay, I will stay. Your people will be my people and your God my God. Where you die I will die, and there I will be buried. May the Lord deal with me, be it ever so severely, if anything but death separates you and me."

That was the Scripture! The next day John packed his bags and moved from Texas to California, where he saw Mildred in person for the first time. They were married the next day. Lauren told me that they never spent any significant time apart, up until the day Mildred died. When that happened, John's life was changed forever. As sad as it was to witness his mental and emotional distress over the loss of his wife, Lauren said that is exactly what she hopes to have one day: a marriage and family like her grandparents, John and Mildred.

Just a Piece of Paper?

Have you ever taken a good, hard look at a one-dollar bill? Have you really looked at the color of the ink, the feel and smell of the paper, the shape and the size, and read the year it was minted and the words printed on it—"In God We Trust"?

When I'm speaking in an assembly, I often ask students, "Who has a one-dollar bill easily accessible?" There's usually one young guy who pulls a crinkled bill out of his front pocket and makes his way down to the front of the stage.

I ask if what he's holding has value, and the guy always says yes. Then I hand him a $20 bill—or if I'm in a generous mood, I pull out a C-note—and ask him to analyze it.

"What does it smell, feel and look like?" I'll ask.

The answer is usually, "The same as the one-dollar bill."

"If you had to choose between your bill and my bill, which would you pick?" I ask. Of course, he wants the larger bill!

But my next question is, "Why would you want my bill? After all, isn't it just a piece of paper?"

The Naked Truth is that one piece of paper has greater value than the other. People have been known to mug little old ladies, rob banks and steal others' identities to acquire money, which at the end of the day is "just a piece of paper." The larger the number written on the paper, the more it is valued. That's why some people counterfeit: If they can't earn it, why not copy it?

Now, we know money gets respect, but what about other paper? Try presenting your favorite Pokemon card to the Highway Patrol when he asks you for your driver's license, registration and insurance. Let's see how far you get.

Or how about going to the state lottery officials to collect the $87 million jackpot with the card you made for your mom on Mother's Day in the second grade? How much cash do you think you'll collect with it? You guessed it—*nada*!

The reason some forms of paper command respect and esteem is that their value has a direct relationship with an object or activity. Paper money issued by the government represents something of real value, such as gold or silver. A lottery ticket and its numbers are related to the jackpot. A registration tells the policeman your relationship to the car you're driving, and your license tells him that you have been deemed a legal driver by your state.

My marriage license, though it's printed on a piece of paper, has value because it defines my relationship to the man I sleep with every night as *wife*—not wifee, shortee, friend with benefits, significant other, partner, or anything else. This paper says we are legal and legitimate, and we are driving this life together.

Given the choice, most people will choose items of greater value over lesser ones—or will they? Why is this true about other forms of paper but not about the marriage license, which gets about as much respect as toilet paper these days?

When I shared with an acquaintance in the entertainment business that I was getting married, he remarked, "Why in the world would you want to do a thing like that? You should just live together . . . after all, *marriage is just a piece of paper*."

Today, living together has become a popular counterfeit to marriage and one of the most deceptive lies in truth's clothing. The wedding day is documented with more than beautiful photos—it's sealed by a piece of paper called a marriage license, and The Naked Truth is that it's not just *any* piece of paper.

The marriage license represents a marriage, which is the cornerstone of bringing people together in a family. Marriage is a social institution that has been tested and reaffirmed countless times over thousands of years and is deeply rooted in every society around the world. When marriages and families are healthy, communities thrive—and when marriages break down, communities break down.

The Naked Truth is that a marriage license isn't just *any* piece of paper.

Former First Lady Hillary Rodham Clinton popularized the African proverb, "It takes a village to raise a child." However true this may be, the corresponding African proverb was completely ignored by her and the press: "The ruin of any nation begins in its homes."

Marriage is the means to a stable and enduring family, but it has taken a backseat to cohabitating (also known as shacking up or living together). Since the sexual revolution of the 1960s, many people have come to view marriage as an old-fashioned, outdated institution that has no relevance in modern American culture. Many view marriage as "just a piece of paper."

In 1930, married couples accounted for 84 percent of households in the U.S. By 1990, that number had declined to about 56 percent. In 2005, it slipped to 49 percent.—U.S. Census American Community Survey[1]

The idea that living together before marriage is an equally beneficial or even better option than marriage is flat wrong. This may come across to some as an arrogant statement, but facts—like a DNA paternity test—don't lie. Since the 1970s, marriages that began with cohabitation have skyrocketed from 10 percent to 56 percent.

Recent surveys of men and women show that the majority of single young adults in metropolitan cities favor cohabitation before marriage. Almost 60 percent of high school seniors agreed with the statement, "It is usually a good idea for a couple to live together before getting married in order to find out whether they really get along."[2] This lie in truth's clothing couldn't be farther from the truth. Research shows that cohabitation does not lead to increased *or even equal* satisfaction or stability once a couple gets married. Compared to marriage, cohabitation creates disadvantages for individuals, couples and children.[3]

> *It's the legacy of the Boomers that has finally caused this tipping point. Certainly later generations have followed in Boomer footsteps, with high levels of living together before marriage and more flexible lifestyles. But the Boomers were the trailblazers, once again rebelling against a norm their parents epitomized . . . This would seem to close the book on the Ozzie and Harriet era that characterized much of the last century.*—William H. Frey, demographer, Brookings Institution[4]

Our culture has developed such a cynicism toward marriage that it's no wonder the majority of people I talk to in my peer group say that they no longer value marriage. Yet I have found that they don't necessarily hate marriage or find it undesirable. If the truth be told, they have a secret fantasy to find a "happily ever after" kind of love, but they don't know where to find it or how to keep it, and question if it really exists in the first place. A close friend of mine idolizes marriage yet lives with his significant other, lamenting that he'll probably never find his soul mate. He says, "I'm not afraid of marriage. I'm just terrified of divorce."

> "For the first time in our nation's history, marriage has become a minority status." –U.S. Census American Community Survey[5]

I can understand why some of my peers may be gun-shy or resistant toward the concept, especially when the adults in their lives have had less than exemplary marriages. The majority of people my age and younger will be casualties of divorced parents or will be raised by a single parent who never married. I know that if I didn't have my grandparents as role models, the only example of marriage I would have had would have been tired reruns of *The Brady Bunch*–and how real is that?

Let's take a look at why people choose living together over marriage, explore why cohabitating doesn't work and consider the better alternative: marriage.

Why People Choose to Live Together and Why It Doesn't Work

The lie that marriage is just a piece of paper is usually cloaked in other common little lies. They are so cliché that nobody questions them anymore, and most people miss what is really being said.

Convenience

It's just so much more convenient for us to live together. I mean, it's less expensive to share rent and utilities than to pay for two. Besides, it's easier not to have to carry my overnight bag back and forth all the time.

This is just another way of saying, "I want you to carry my baggage so that I don't have to be responsible . . . and if anything should go wrong, I can just leave you holding the bag—or the bills."

To a female, this trial run is a naïve hope that her live-in boyfriend will eventually see it her way and commit to marriage—but studies show that the longer they live together, the more negative his (and perhaps even her) attitude about marriage and childbearing will be.[6] She may hope for a wedding, but odds are she'll be disappointed in what's really coming—the relationship between living together and eventual divorce is very strong.[7]

Individuals who choose to cohabitate often develop a relatively low tolerance for unhappiness and a greater willingness to quit relationships, including marriage, because they have established a pattern of leaving rather than choosing to work through differences.[8] (For further clarification, I recommend you watch a few episodes of *Judge Judy*. She does a much better job of explaining why single people should not shack up than I ever could, considering that she's been sitting on the bench as a judge longer than I have been alive.)

Moreover, the breakup of a cohabiting relationship is not necessarily cleaner or easier than a divorce. Any breakup that involves splitting up a household may lead to conflicts over property, leases, and past due bills, bills, bills.[9] Just ask Judge Judy. If you've never seen her dispense justice to the victims of a live-in situation gone bad, let me tell you—it's never good! Being house-mates and being spouse-mates are not the same under the law.

Sexual Compatibility

I think we need to see if we're sexually compatible.

Compatibility? Are people still using this tired old line? First of all, if this person approaches you and you have any hopes of the two of you ever getting married, forget it! Your beloved's obsession with sexual "compatibility" reveals that he or she is more likely to have a negative attitude about marriage and in the long run is more likely to accept divorce as a solution to marriage problems.[10]

Second, if they are basing a marriage on whether or not the sex is good, they aren't a good marriage candidate—to say the least. Someone who makes such a dumb statement with regard to marriage hasn't the faintest idea what marriage is all about. Married people spend much more time doing life than doing *it*. Compatibility is a choice.

When it comes to compatibility, I like to say, "Read the box before you buy your software." Will it function with your hardware and operating system? This is all you need to know, and all that information is printed on the package. I can hear you asking now, "Why buy the software when I can download it for free?" Because free downloads are how you get viruses.

Test Driving, a.k.a. "Practice"

I think living together 24/7 is good practice to see if we get along, without having to be trapped in a marriage if it doesn't work. It's just not smart to buy a car without test driving it.

The fear of commitment is rampant these days. I know commitment can be a scary thing—especially if you've been burned before—but equating living together and test driving (or even leasing!) a car is just wacked. It's a bad metaphor. No car dealer in his right mind would let you go four-wheeling in the Sahara or drag-racing on the Autobahn in a car you haven't paid for yet—and the high-speed extreme sport of living with another person makes four-wheeling or drag-racing look like a trip on a merry-go-round. Marriage is like owning a Rolls with the speed of a LOTUS and the safety of a Volvo. Don't settle for test driving a Geo Metro. It just won't get you very far.

The sad reality is that cohabitants feel less secure in their relationships than married couples because they view their sexual relationships as less permanent and exclusive. They are less faithful to their partners than spouses. Even when they are faithful, they are less committed to sexual fidelity, which creates more insecurity because "levels of certainty about the relationship are lower than in marriage."[11]

Marriage means "I will always be here for you." Marriage encourages emotional investment in an exclusive relationship. In contrast, cohabitation means, "I will be here only as long as the relationship meets my needs." Contrary to popular belief, the majority of live-ins don't lead to marriage! Only an estimated 60 percent end in marriage.[12] Those who are afraid of commitment and permanence—or who fear that these qualities can no longer be found in marriage—may settle for cohabitation, but they are likely to discover they have settled for less. Couples who live together before marriage are 46 percent more likely to divorce than people who marry but never lived together.[13] No one has ever found that cohabitation makes a positive contribution to later marital stability, regardless of what you see on the latest sitcom.

If failed marriages and relationships aren't enough to prove that living together is high-risk and low-benefit, check this out: Cohabiting women are more likely than married women to be the victims of physical and/or sexual abuse. Some estimate domestic violence is at least twice and as much as three times as common among live-in couples as it is among married people.[14]

I talk regularly with casualties of cohabitation. Kathy, a cute high school sophomore, confided in me after an all-school assembly that she loved the abstinence message and wanted to embrace secondary virginity. She thought it was a great idea and she hoped to find an example of a good marriage. Her parents were high school sweethearts but never got married. She and her sister had only seen their biological dad twice.

She told me, "I really want to share this message with my mom, but I don't think her boyfriend is going to like it."

"Who cares what he thinks," I challenged her. "She has to do what's best for her and her children."

"You're right," she said, "but her boyfriend lives with us and he's kind of abusive."

At this point I thought to myself, *Here we go again . . . same story, different girl.* As we talked further, she began to reveal the dark secrets of her life, which unfortunately fit perfectly into the statistical profile of a child of cohabitation.

This young woman and her sister were both molested by one of her mom's previous live-in boyfriends, and when her sister told the mother, she didn't do anything about it. Some women think that living with someone will help in the raising of their children, but cohabitation increases the chances that a child—male or female—will be abused. Boyfriends are disproportionately likely to sexually or physically abuse their girlfriend's children. In fact, the most unsafe family environment for children is when the mother is living with someone other than the child's biological father.[15]

The abuse, as you can imagine, heaped a great amount of emotional distress on both this young woman and her sister. She told me that she wanted to go to college, but her mom didn't have the money. She didn't know where her father was, and she had no right to support from any of her mother's previous "partners" who were not her biological father. She and her sister paid the economic price for her mother's life.

"Your grades aren't that good, are they?" I asked.

"How did you know?" she responded with surprise.

I knew because it's the same sad story I've heard too many times to count. This girl wasn't getting low grades because she wasn't bright, but because she was experimenting with alcohol and sex to emotionally escape her situation at home. She seemed very bright and extremely mature for her age, but her mother's poor decisions had caused her to have behavioral problems and lower academic performance than children in married families.

Marriage: The Best Alternative

I truly believe countless lives would change for the better if people were told The Naked Truth about the benefits of marriage. Families could not continue to be in such disarray if true believers—not make-believers—began to evangelize their communities about marriage. It's important to share what God says, but it's more powerful to live the truth. How you live your life says more about you than anything you can ever say. A marriage revival will only occur when Christians obey God's charge in 2 Chronicles 7:14: "If my people, who are called by my name, will humble themselves and pray and seek my face and turn from their wicked ways, then . . . I will heal their land."

> *Evangelize at all times, and when necessary use words.*
> —St. Francis of Assisi

Sex in America was a book that documented the most exhaustive research study ever done on married couples in the U.S. and it found that married people achieve the five basic things that almost everyone wants: long life, health, financial security, sense of well-being, and a happy sex life. Though living together is now generally accepted, its outcomes can't compare to the benefits of marriage.[16]

Married people not only feel better but are actually physically healthier and live longer than single people.[17] There are many mental and physical health benefits to knowing that there is another person who will take care of you when you cannot take care of yourself. Married people vow to care for each other "in sickness and in health, as long we both shall live."

Married couples—who are mutually dependent upon each other, helping each other to meet their financial and career goals—are more likely to be financially responsible for their partners than live-ins, who place a greater value on their independence over dependability. Live-ins are more likely to control their own finances and protect their individual economic futures by having separate bank accounts, instead of working as an economic team.

Married men earn nearly twice as much as single men. This may be explained by the increased financial responsibility men feel when they marry as many men have been heard saying, "Marriage made me get more serious about my career and making a good living."[18]

Married women also benefit from marriage in that they make more money than their cohabitating or single sisters, and they also have access to more of their man's earnings. In addition, many married women report receiving considerable support from their husbands in their careers.[19]

Married couples are also better off financially because they monitor each other's spending in a way that emphasizes "*our* budget." For most marrieds, "Your money is my money, and my money is your money." According to the authors of *The Case for Marriage*, "This financial union is one of the cornerstones (along with sexual union) of what Americans mean by marriage."[20]

Finally, married people are emotionally happier on the whole than singles, and they have more stable and secure relationships within their communities.[21]

In some families, cohabitation is no longer cause for parental disapproval. But in many families, cohabitation is still immoral and embarrassing to extended family members. Live-ins from these families run the risk of damaging their relationships with parents and experiencing the withdrawal of parental and extended family support for the relationship. Additionally, the temporary nature of live-in relationships may limit access to grandparents for children who might end up switching sets of grandparents multiple times.

People who live together may seem to have achieved the same benefits as married couples, but those benefits vanish in the long run and they are no better off than singles.[22] Because cohabiting relationships are temporary by nature, the benefits last for a relatively short time, and if the couple splits up rather than marrying, the benefits are lost at a high emotional and psychological cost very similar to what people experience in a divorce.[23]

Surprise! The vast majority of people might be surprised to learn that married couples have better sex lives than couples who are shacking up. Because marriage is the capstone of commitment in the relationship, it adds a deeper sense of internal security to one's sex life. Married couples are more likely to perceive love and sex as intrinsically connected. This makes sex between married couples essentially more satisfying because the spouse's intentions and commitment is not in question. Don't get me wrong: Live-ins are having sex just about as often as married couples—but they are less likely to say they enjoy it as much as married couples do.[24]

It is often hard to distinguish between a lie in truth's clothing and truth itself, so it's no wonder why living together can appear to be like marriage: shared living space, diminished cost of living, convenient sex, even having and raising children together. I often hear, "We are just as committed as any married couple" . . . but the numbers don't lie. Studies show a lower level of commitment between these couples, less dedication to the continuation of the relationship and less willingness to sacrifice to preserve the relationship. Moreover, these couples report lower levels of happiness, less sexual fidelity, more sexual dissatisfaction and poorer relationships with their parents.

Living together as a married couple is not an effective trial marriage. It does not provide divorce insurance and cannot compete with the rewards and benefits of a strong, committed marriage. Couples are better off in life's measures of success and happiness (emotional health, physical health, personal wealth, general happiness and longevity) if they are married rather than living together. People need to know that Satan's counterfeit of living together fails to bring couples the happiness and stability they desire in a close intimate relationship. Shackin' fails to reap the benefits of marriage.

The current generation of young adults longs for satisfying and stable relationships that provide the essential things in life: long life, health, financial stability, a sense of well-being, and a happy sex life. Unfortunately, our American culture has deceived many into believing that they can achieve these things without engaging in the divine rite of passage called marriage. Some have accepted the flawed counterfeit known as shacking up, living together or cohabitating, and those who have chosen to adhere to God's ordained union called marriage have become anxious about their ability to achieve it in a cynical, media-saturated world.

Their fears will be calmed through better premarriage education and counseling. The alternatives to marriage appear reasonable and attractive but will prove faulty over time and fail when compared to marriage. Educators, premarriage counselors, the Church, the media and parents must begin to proclaim the divine institution of marriage as essential to personal and family success. *The Case for Marriage* reminds us, "Support for marriage . . . does not require turning back the clock on desirable social change, promoting male tyranny, or tolerating domestic violence . . . Whether an individual ever personally marries or not, a healthy marriage culture benefits every [person]."[25]

There is a movement among young people across the nation. True Love Waits, The National Abstinence Clearinghouse, Club Varsity, and other organizations have led millions of youth to pledge to wait for sex until after they are married. These young adults have rejected the lies in truth's clothing that many of their peers accept as the norm:

- It can't happen to me.
- I'll just practice "safe sex."
- It (pregnancy) just happened.
- They're gonna do it anyway.
- What two people do behind closed doors is nobody else's business.
- I only listen to the beat.
- Sex is a natural bodily function that can't be controlled.
- Peer pressure/Everybody's doing it.
- It's too late for me.
- Marriage is just a piece of paper.

The Word says that Satan often appears as an angel of light, cloaked in truth's clothing. The Deceiver is like a mirage, holding out empty promises that will disappear and even lead you away from fulfilling the hopes you have for your life.

Not everyone who abstains from sex until marriage always lives happily ever after. But those who choose to live as God intended in the area of sexuality avoid the wide road that ultimately leads to death and destruction (STDs and AIDS, unplanned pregnancy, abortion, illegitimate births, divorce, etc.). Those who decide to follow God and not the world have chosen the narrow road, which promises life and peace.

When I hold up a hundred dollar bill while speaking, I ask the audience, "Who wants this?" The majority of people sit waving their hands around, shouting, "Me! Me! I want that!" But the person who gets to keep it:

1. Sees the opportunity
   Know the options and the consequences.
2. Makes the decision to get up out of his or her chair
   Make a decision.
3. Ignores what their peers are, or aren't, doing
   Find others who will support your decision.
4. Comes down to the front and pulls it out of my hand
   Plan and act.

The Naked Truth is that wanting something is not enough. If you really want it, you've got to get up and do something about it. Whatever choice you make, begin with the end in mind. That means, choose today whom to serve! All we have to do is open up the Bible to Proverbs 3:16 to discover that "the fear of the Lord will give you long life, riches, honor, pleasure and peace." It is the best opportunity for lasting happiness for you, for your children and for the generations to come.

And that is The Naked Truth.

Ask Yourself

- Why is marriage so much more than a piece of paper?
- What do you think your wedding day will look like?
- What do you think your marriage will look like?
- Why is marriage worth waiting for when it comes to sex?

APPENDIX

Self-Defense Manual

Prevention is the best protection! That's why abstaining from sex until marriage and tying the knot with an uninfected mate is the best and only safe sex. If you have had sexual intercourse in the past, you should be tested for STDs, and if you've already experienced symptoms, seek medical treatment immediately. Some STDs can be easily apprehended and cured once detected, but if damage has already occurred, it cannot be reversed.

There are no home remedies or over-the-counter drugs for STDs. A physician can provide penicillin or other antibiotics to treat bacterial STDs, but viral STDs such as HIV/AIDS and Hepatitis B can never be completely cured. Early detection, however, allows options for treatment and preventive measures that can increase your length and quality of life. Here's how to defend yourself from America's Most Unwanted.

Chlamydia

"Actual use" studies of condoms show that using condoms probably reduces the risk of Chlamydia among sexually active people but does not consistently prevent against infection.

Gonorrhea

If used consistently and correctly, condoms may help reduce the risk of contracting gonorrhea. Sexually active individuals, especially those at high risk for contracting this disease, should be screened and treated each time they change sexual partners to prevent long-term complications and to prevent spreading infection to others.

Hepatitis B

Studies are lacking, but given the way Hepatitis B is communicated, condoms can only be expected to reduce–not eliminate–the risk of infection. Vaccinations are now available to all ages for prevention. If you shoot drugs intravenously or received a body piercing or tattoo with a contaminated instrument, however, you may be at risk regardless of the vaccine.

Herpes
Condoms don't cover all the skin in the genital area, and sex with an infected partner can result in herpes infection because the virus is transmitted through skin-to-skin contact. Based on limited studies, condoms appear to reduce the risk of contracting genital herpes by only half at best.

HIV/AIDS
If you don't shoot drugs and haven't had sex, you don't have to worry about contracting HIV/AIDS. The perfect use of condoms can reduce the chance of infection by 85 percent.[1] (Wow! With only a measly 15 percent chance of contracting a deadly virus, where do I sign up?)

HPV
Since HPV is so common, those who become sexually active outside of marriage are likely to become infected by the virus, even if they use plastic protection. Condoms don't cover all the skin in the genital area, and HPV is communicated by skin-to-skin contact.

Syphilis
Through perfect usage of condoms, you may reduce your chances of contracting syphilis by 30 to 50 percent.[2] But remember that it's easily transmitted through oral sex, too!

Trichomonas
Trichomonas is transmitted through the exchange of bodily fluids, so condoms may reduce the risk of infection—however, as with other STDs, condoms provide incomplete protection.

The Crabs
Pubic lice don't give a rip about a condom. They are miniscule little creatures that hide out in pubic hairs. If you don't want them, zip it up, lock it down and sign up for the Clank! security system!

The Naked Truth is that even if you engage in "protected" sex, you still have a significant chance of contracting an STD. It's also possible to become infected with any of these STDs, including HIV/AIDS, through oral sex. If you have already been sexually active outside of marriage, talk to your physician or health care provider about getting tested for STDs, and encourage anyone you have had sex with to do the same. Abstinence from sexual activity (including oral and anal sex) or marriage to an uninfected mate is the only 100 percent guaranteed way to avoid being infected—and that is The Naked Truth.

Endnotes

Chapter 2: The Naked Truth

1. Y. Shoda, W. Mischel and P.K. Peake, "Predicting Adolescent Cognitive and Self-regulatory Competencies from Preschool Delay of Gratification: Identifying Diagnostic Conditions," *Developmental Psychology,* November 1990:26(6), pp. 978-86.

Chapter 3: It Can't Happen to Me

1. Denise Holfers, et al., "Adolescent Depression and Suicide Risk: Association with Sex and Drug Behavior," *American Journal of Preventive Medicine,* 2004: 27(3). Robert E. Rector, Kirk A. Johnson, Ph.D., Lauren R. Noyes and Shannan Martin, *The Harmful Effects of Early Sexual Activity and Multiple Sexual Partners Among Women: A Book of Charts* (Washington, D.C.: The Heritage Foundation, 2004).
2. Rector, Johnson, Noyes and Martin, *The Harmful Effects of Early Sexual Activity and Multiple Sexual Partners Among Women: A Book of Charts.*
3. Holfers, et al., "Adolescent Depression and Suicide Risk: Association with Sex and Drug Behavior." Rector, Johnson, Noyes and Martin, *The Harmful Effects of Early Sexual Activity and Multiple Sexual Partners Among Women: A Book of Charts.*
4. T.R. Eng and W.T. Butler, eds. *The Hidden Epidemic—Confronting Sexually Transmitted Disease* (Washington, D.C: National Academy Press, 1997).
5. Ibid.
6. Ibid.
7. "Genital Herpes—CDC Fact Sheet," Department of Health and Human Services Centers for Disease Control and Prevention, May 2004. http://www.cdc.gov/std/Herpes/STDFact-Herpes.htm#common (accessed December 2006).
8. Meg Meeker, *Epidemic: How Teen Sex Is Killing Our Kids* (Washington, D.C.: Regnery Publishing Company, 2002), p. 12.
9. Joyce A. Martin, MPH, Brady E. Hamilton, Ph.D., Paul D. Sutton, Ph.D., et al, "National Vital Statistics Reports; Births: Final Data for 2002," National Center for Health Statistics, December 17, 2003:52(10). http://www.cdc.gov/nchs/ data/nvsr/nvsr52/nvsr52_10.pdf (accessed April 2004).
10. D.J. Landry and J.D. Forrest, "How Old Are U.S. Fathers?" *Family Planning Perspectives,* 1995 (27), 159-161. "California Vital Statistics Section 1992; California Residents' Live Births, 1990, by Age of Mother, Age of Father, Race, Marital Status," California Department of Health Services (Sacramento, CA: California Department of Health Services, 1992).
11. Ed Oliver, "Parents Are Well Equipped to Protect Kids from STD Epidemic," MassNews.com, April 16, 2003.
12. "In Da Club," © 2003 by 50 Cent Music (Universal Music Corporation), Los Angeles, CA. All rights reserved.

Chapter 5: I'll Just Practice Safe Sex

1. "Condoms," AIDS Policy and Law, Vol. 18, No. 13 (July 22, 2003).
2. "Workshop Summary: Scientific Evidence on Condom Effectiveness for Sexually Transmitted Disease (STD) Prevention," National Institute of Allergy and Infectious Diseases, National Institutes of Health, July 20, 2001. http://www.fda.gov/ohrms/DOCKETS/dockets/04n0556/04n-0556-EC28-Attach-1.pdf.
3. On December 12, 1994, U.S. Surgeon General Joycelyn Elders was fired from her position because of the controversy that erupted around her support for the

public discussion of masturbation as an appropriate topic in school sexual education programs. See "Masturbation: From Stigma to Sexual Health," Planned Parenthood® Federation of America, Inc., November 2002. http://www4.plannedparenthood.org/pp2/portal/files/portal/medicalinfo/sexualhealth/white-020904-masturbation.pdf (accessed December 2006).

4. H. Fu, J. E. Darroch, T. Haas and N. Ranjit, "Contraceptive Failure Rates: New Estimates from the 1995 National Survey of Family Growth," *Family Planning Perspective,* 1999:31, pp. 56-63.
5. "Workshop Summary: Scientific Evidence on Condom Effectiveness for Sexually Transmitted Disease (STD) Prevention," National Institute of Allergy and Infectious Diseases, National Institutes of Health, July 20, 2001. http://www.fda.gov/ohrms/DOCKETS/dockets/04n0556/04n-0556-EC28-Attach-1.pdf (accessed December 2006).
6. "What Is HPV?" Cervical Cancer Campaign. http://www.cervicalcancercampaign.org/faqs.aspx (accessed December 2006).
7. "What Causes Cervical Cancer?" University of Maryland Medical Center, September 20, 2002. http://www.umm.edu/patiented/articles/what_causes_cervical_cancer_000046_3.htm (accessed December 2006).
8. What Is HPV?" Cervical Cancer Campaign. http://www.cervicalcancercampaign.org/faqs.aspx (accessed December 2006).
9. Centers for Disease Control Responses to Questions on HPV and Cervical Cancer from the Subcommittee on Health and Environment, April 2, 1999.
10. K. K. Holmes, R. Levine and M. Weaver, "Effectiveness of Condoms in Preventing Sexually Transmitted Infections," *Bull World Health Organization,* June 2004, 82(6): pp. 454-461. J. Shepherd, G. Peersman, R. Weston and I. Napuli, "Cervical Cancer and Sexual Lifestyle: Systematic Review of Health Education Interventions Targeted at Women," *Health Education Resources,* December 15, 2000, 15(6): pp. 681-694. L. E. Manhart and L. A. Koustsky, "Do Condoms Prevent Genital HPV Infection, External Genital Warts, or Cervical Neoplasia? A Meta-analysis," *Sexually Transmitted Diseases,* November 2002, 29(11), pp. 725-735. R. L. Winer, S. K. Lee, J. P. Hughes, et al, "Genital Human Papillomavirus Infection: Incidence and Risk Factors in a Cohort of Female University Students," *American Journal of Epidemiology,* May 1, 2003, 157(9), p. 858.
11. Dr. Nancy C. Lee, Director, Division of Cancer Prevention and Control, Centers for Disease Control and Prevention, Testimony Before the Subcommittee on Health Environment Hearing on Women's Health: Raising Awareness of Cervical Cancer, March 16, 1999, Hearing Serial No. 106-4. http://www.siecus.org/policy/PUpdates/arch00/arch000031.html (accessed November 2006).
12. "Prevalence" is a measure of the proportion of people in a population affected with a disease at a given time. "Incidence" is the number of new cases of a disease occurring in a given population over a certain period.
13. Tom Carter, "Uganda Leads by Example on AIDS," *The Washington Times*, March 13, 2003.
14. Edward C. Green, Ph.D., Harvard Center for Population and Development Studies, Testimony Before the Subcommittee on African Affairs, Committee on Foreign Relations, U.S. Senate, May 19, 2003.
15. Emily Wax, "Ugandans Say Facts, Not Abstinence, Will Win AIDS War," *The Washington Post*, July 9, 2003.

Chapter 7: What Two People Do Behind Closed Doors . . .

1. H. W. Chesson, J. M. Blandford, T. L. Gift, G. Tao and K. L. Irwin, "The Estimated Direct Medical Cost of STDs Among American Youth, 2000," Abstract P075, 2004 National STD Prevention Conference, Philadelphia, PA, March 8-11, 2004.
2. R. L. Coley and P. L. Chase-Lansdale, "Adolescent Pregnancy and Parenthood: Recent Evidence and Future Directions," *American Psychology*, 1998, 53(2), pp. 152-166.
3. U.S. General Accounting Office, "Teen Mothers: Selected Socio-Demographic Characteristics and Risk Factors," Washington, DC: U.S. General Accounting Office, June 1998, GAO/HEHS-98-141. http://www.hi-ho.ne.jp/taku77/refer/teenmo.pdf (accessed August 2005).
4. Dawn MacKeen, "Cassanovas Who Kill," *Mothers Who Think*, November 10, 1997. http://www.salon.com/mwt/hot/1997/11/10hot.html (accessed November 2006).
5. Geraldo Rivera, CNBC telecast, September 7, 1997. http://www.actupny.org/alert/Nushawn-TV.html (accessed December 2006).
6. MacKeen, "Cassanovas Who Kill," from *Mothers Who Think* (accessed November 28, 2006).
7. "Teens More Knowledgeable–but Not Necessarily More Careful–One Year After Nushawn Williams," *Boston Globe Online,* October 29, 1998. http://www.aegis.org/news/ads/1998/AD982094.html (accessed December 2006).

Chapter 8: It Just Happened

1. Chris Rock, *Never Scared.* © 2005 Dreamworks, Los Angeles, CA. All rights reserved.

Chapter 9: I Just Listen to the Beat

1. Lindsey Tanner, "Sexual Lyrics Prompt Teens to Have Sex, *SFGate.com,* August 6, 2006. http://www.sfgate.com/cgi-in/article.cgi?f=/n/a/2006/08/06/national/a215010D94.DTL (accessed December 2006).
2. Ibid.
3. S. Liliana Escobar-Chaves, "The Impact of the Media on Adolescent Sexual Attitudes and Behaviors," *Pediatrics,* July 2005, 116(1), p. 2. "Does Watching Sex on Television Influence Teens' Sexual Activity?" Rand Corporation, 2004. http://www.rand.org/pubs/research_briefs/RB9068/index1.html (accessed December 2006).
4. Martin Peers, "Buddy, Can You Spare Some Time?" *EWSJ,* January 26, 2004, p. B1.
5. Richard Pellegrino MD, quoted in *Billboard* magazine, January 23, 1999.
6. David Tame, *The Secret Power of Music* (Shippensburg, PA: Destiny Books, 1984), p. 15.
7. "Rand Study Finds Adolescents Who Listen to a Great Deal of Music with Degrading Sexual Lyrics Have Sex Sooner," Rand Corporation, August 7, 2006. http://www.rand.org/news/press.06/08.07.html.
8. Carl Jeffrey Wright, *God's Vision or Television* (Calumet City, IL: Urban Ministries, Inc., 2004), p. 14.
9. Jerry Armor, "Snoop Dogg Explains Slang in New Song," Yahoo Launch, November 26, 2002.
10. Snoop Dogg, "Bo$$ Playa," © 2002 Priority Records. http://www.metrolyrics.com/lyrics/217418/Snoop_Dogg/Bo$$_Playa (accessed December 2006).
11. Interview with Marilyn Manson, *Kerrang* magazine, November 27, 1999.
12. Oprah Winfrey, quoted in an interview with Mary J. Blige, February 1, 2006.
13. Chris Rock, *Never Scared,* HBO Comedy Event, April 17, 2004.
14. Daniel Low-Beer and Rand L. Stoneburner, "Behavior and Communication Change in Reducing HIV: Is Uganda Unique?" *African Journal of AIDS Research*, vol. 3, 2003. Low-Beer, who formerly worked for the World Health Organization in its

HIV surveillance unit, studies behavior and communication change in relation to HIV in East and Southern Africa. Stoneburner is an epidemiologist who has worked with the Centers for Disease Control and the World Health Organization. See also David Wilson, "The 'ABCs' of HIV Prevention: Report of a U.S.AID Technical Meeting on Behavior Change Approaches to Primary Prevention of HIV/AIDS," U.S. Agency for International Development, September 17, 2002.

Chapter 11: It's Too Late for Me

1. "Americans Sound Off About Teen Pregnancy," National Campaign to Prevent Teen Pregnancy, December 2003, p. 17.

Chapter 12: Marriage Is Just a Piece of Paper

1 Sam Roberts, "To Be Married Means to Be Outnumbered," *New York Times*, October 15, 2006.
2. J. G. Bachman, L. D. Johnston and P. M. O'Malley, *Monitoring the Future: Questionnaire Responses from the Nation's High School Seniors, 2000.*
3. Nock, 1995; Brown and Booth, 1996 and Linda J. Waite and Kara Joyner, "Emotional and Physical Satisfaction with Sex in Married, Cohabiting, and Dating Sexual Unions: Do Men and Women Differ?" cited in Edward O. Laumann and Robert T. Michaels, eds., *Sex, Love, and Health in America* (Chicago, IL: University of Chicago Press, 2001), pp. 239-269. Judith Treas and Deirdre Giesen, "Sexual Infidelity Among Married and Cohabiting Americans," *Journal of Marriage and the Family,* 2000, 62, pp. 48-60. Renate Forste and Koray Tanfer, "Sexual Exclusivity Among Dating, Cohabiting, and Married Women," *Journal of Marriage and the Family,* 1996, 58, pp. 33-47. Paul R. Amato and Alan Booth, *A Generation at Risk* (Cambridge, MA: Harvard University Press, 1997), Table 4-2, p. 258.
4. Sam Roberts, "To Be Married Means to Be Outnumbered," *New York Times,* October 15, 2006.
5. Ibid.
6. Jeffry H. Larson, *Should We Stay Together? A Scientifically Proven Method for Evaluating Your Relationship and Improving Its Chances for Long-term Success* (San Francisco: Jossey-Bass, 2000), note 5. For additional information, visit http://marriageandfamilies.byu.edu/issues/2001/January/cohabitation.aspx.
7. David Popenoe and Barbara Dafoe Whitehead, "Should We Live Together? What Young Adults Need to Know about Cohabitation Before Marriage: A Comprehensive Review of Recent Research." http://marriage.rutgers.edu/Publications/Print/PrintSWLT.htm (accessed December 2006).
8. Linda J. Waite and Maggie Gallagher, *The Case for Marriage: Why Married People Are Happier, Healthier and Better Off Financially* (New York: Doubleday Books, 2000).
9. Ibid.
10. Ibid.
11. Ibid.
12. Linda J. Waite and K. Joyner, "Emotional and Physical Satisfaction in Married, Cohabiting and Dating Sexual Unions: Do Men and Women differ?" cited in E. O. Laumann and R. Michael, eds., *Studies in Sex* (Chicago, IL: University of Chicago, 1994).
13. David Popenoe and Barbara Dafoe Whitehead, *Should We Live Together? What Young Adults Need to Know About Cohabitation Before Marriage* (New Brunswick, NJ: The National Marriage Project, 1999), note 4.
14. Waite and Gallagher, *The Case for Marriage: Why Married People Are Happier, Healthier and Better Off Financially,* p. 41, note 6.

15. R. Whelan, *Broken Homes and Battered Children: A Study of the Relationship Between Child Abuse and Family Type* (London: Family Education Trust, 1993).
16. Lee A. Lillard and Linda J. Waite, "Till Death Do Us Part: Marital Disruption and Mortality," *American Journal of Sociology,* 1995, 100, pp. 1131-1156. R. Jay Turner and Franco Marino, "Social Support and Social Structure: A Descriptive Epidemiology," *Journal of Health and Social Behavior,* 1994, 35, pp. 193-212. Linda J. Waite, "Does Marriage Matter?" *Demography,* 1995, (32)4, pp. 483-507. Sanders Korenman and David Neumark, "Does Marriage Really Make Men More Productive?" *The Journal of Human Resources,* 1990, (26)2, pp. 282-307. George A. Akerlof, "Men Without Children," *The Economic Journal,* 1998, 108, pp. 287-309.
17. Popenoe and Whitehead, *Should We Live Together? What Young Adults Need to Know About Cohabitation Before Marriage,* note 4.
18. Linda J. Waite, "Does Marriage Matter?" *Demography,* 1995, 32, pp. 483-507.
19. C. E. Ross, J. Mirowski and K. Goldsteen, "The Impact of the Family on Health: The Decade in Review," *Journal of Marriage and the Family,* 1990, 52, pp. 1059-1078.
20. Waite and Gallagher, *The Case for Marriage: Why Married People Are Happier, Healthier and Better Off Financially,* note 6.
21. Ibid.
22. Popenoe and Whitehead, *Should We Live Together? What Young Adults Need to Know About Cohabitation Before Marriage,* note 4.
23. Waite and Joyner, "Emotional and Physical Satisfaction in Married, Cohabiting and Dating Sexual Unions: Do Men and Women Differ?"
24. "The State of Our Unions 2000: The Social Health of Marriage in America," The National Marriage Project (New Brunswick, NJ: The National Marriage Project, 2000), note 1.
25. Waite and Gallagher, *The Case for Marriage: Why Married People Are Happier, Healthier and Better Off Financially,* note 6.

Appendix: Self-Defense Manual

1. M. Macaluso, J. Kelaghan, L. Artz, et al., "Mechanical Failure of the Latex Condom in a Cohort of Women at High STD Risk," *Sexually Transmitted Diseases,* 1999, 26(8), pp. 450-458.
2. J. M. Baeten, P. M. Nyange, B. A. Richardson, et. al., "Hormonal Contraception and Risk of Transmitted Acquisition: Results from a Prospective Study," *American Journal of Obstetrics and Gynecology*, 2001, 185, pp. 380-385.

More Breakthrough Books from Soul Sister and Soul Survivor

Connect
The Lowdown on Relationships and Friendships
Kendall Payne
ISBN 978.08307.37314

Shine
Beautiful Inside and Out
Aly Hawkins
ISBN 978.08307.37307

Respect
How to Get It, How to Give It
Jessie Minassian
ISBN 978.08307.37994

Soul Survivor
Finding Passion and Purpose in the Dry Places
Mike Pilavachi
ISBN 978.08307.33248

Trust
Surrendering to God and the Importance of Forgiveness
Tammy Vervoorn
ISBN 978.08307.42967

Soul Sister
The Truth About Being God's Girl
Beth Redman
ISBN 978.08307.32128

Available at Bookstores Everywhere!

Visit **www.regalbooks.com** to join **Regal's FREE e-newsletter.** You'll get useful **excerpts from our newest releases** and **special access to online chats with your favorite authors.** Sign up today!

Regal
God's Word for Your World
www.regalbooks.com